DEMOCRACY INVADES ISLAM

All Scripture quotations in this book are taken from the King James Version of the Bible unless otherwise noted.

Democracy Invades Islam

Published by The Olive Press, a subsidiary of Midnight Call, Inc.
West Columbia, South Carolina 29170

Copy Typist:	Lynn Jeffcoat
Copy Editor:	Kimberly Farmer
Proofreaders:	Kimberly Farmer, Kathy Roland and Lynn Jeffcoat
Layout/Design:	Michelle Kim
Cover Design:	Michelle Kim

Library of Congress Cataloging-in-Publication Data

Froese, Arno
Democracy Invades Islam
ISBN #9780937422687

1. Bible—Prophecy 2. Democracy 3. Middle East

Printed in the United States of America

The sole purpose of publishing this book is to encourage the readers to surrender and consecrate their lives to Christ.

All funds received from the sale of this book will be used exclusively for the furtherance of the Gospel.

No one associated with this ministry receives a royalty for any of the literature published by Midnight Call Ministries, Inc.

CONTENTS

Chapter 4
DEMOCRACY AND THE BIBLE 57

Chapter 5
THE JEWS, THE CHURCH AND THE GENTILES 63

Chapter 6

Chapter 7

Chapter 8
ANTICHRIST ON THE HORIZON 99

Chapter 9
WHY THE WORLD MUST CHANGE 107

Chapter 16
THE MASTER DECEIVER AT HIS BEST 199

Chapter 17
THE SHAKING OF THE ARAB NATIONS 217

PREFACE

The pro-democracy uprising in the Arab world is the motivating factor for writing this book. There are innumerable opinions, commentaries, and speculations regarding the reason for this seemingly popular revolution, of which many are very fitting and realistic.

So, why the book? Christians have a different worldview; ours is not based upon nationality, religion, politics or geography. Our view is based on Holy Scripture. We rely on the prophetic Word for the answers to our questions.

First and foremost, the Bible tells us that the world is sinful; that means enemies of God the Creator! Unfortunately, that is a statement the world rejects. Great philosophers, poets and intellectuals have come to the conclusion that there is some good in humanity. But Jesus contradicts that assumption with His words, "There is none good but one, that is, God." Isaiah 40:17 summarizes all of human history, "All nations before him are as nothing; and they are counted to him less than nothing, and vanity."

Nevertheless, that discouraging statement of Holy Scripture is not the end, because John 3:16 says, "For God so loved the world, that he gave his only begotten Son, that whosoever believeth in him should not perish, but have everlasting life."

With this, the Bible identifies two groups of people, "He that believeth on the Son hath everlasting life: and he that believeth not the Son shall not see life; but the wrath of God abideth on him" (John 3:36).

Those who believe in the Son have become new creatures in Christ, constituting a new nation, totally different from all nations on the face of the earth. The Bible says, "They are in the world, but not of the world."

God in His love has not condemned the world without offering His plan of salvation.

That's the point where the enemy of God, Satan, also called the devil and Lucifer, enters the picture. He is the god of this world; he actually owns this world because God says in His Word, "He who sins is of the devil." For that reason, the devil fanatically opposes God's plan of salvation. Jesus said, "Salvation is of the Jews," thus the devil must persecute the Jews and the true Church of Jesus Christ.

Scripture makes it clear that the Church cannot be defeated. Jesus says, "I will build my Church; and the gates of hell shall not prevail against it." Israel's existence is also guaranteed, "Thus saith the LORD, which giveth the sun for a light by day, and the ordinances of the moon and of the stars for a light by night, which divideth the sea when the waves thereof roar; The LORD of hosts is his name: If those ordinances depart from before me, saith the LORD, then the seed of Israel also shall cease from being a nation before me for ever" (Jeremiah 31:35-36).

Thus, the question: how can Satan effectively oppose the Church and Israel? First, he must unify the world to create global peace. Second, He must present himself as the Savior of the world and the Messiah of Israel.

How is he to accomplish this feat? One word: deception. That is the real message of this book. In order for the devil to create peace on earth, goodwill toward men, and to guarantee prosperity to all people, he must bring all nations together. That means world unity is his first aim, politically, economically and religiously.

Here is where democracy comes in. The most respected, beloved and yearned for political system, granting people the right to decide their own future, is doubtless democracy.

While democracy has resulted in relative peace and prosperity throughout the European world (West), the Arab nations have missed out. That is one of the major reasons for the Arab people to revolt against their governments and leaders. Although the Islamic nations are the possessors of the main sources of the world's energy, the population at large is not benefiting from the oil wealth and is overwhelmingly poor.

Now, the time has come for the people to insist on change. In other words, the democracy invasion of the Arab world has begun.

However, the pages of this book show that behind this pro-democracy movement stands the prince of darkness, the god of this world. He is successfully working out the final details in his attempt to establish a one-world society, where all people on earth can live together in peace and harmony. That goal can only be achieved through democracy; thus, the book *Democracy Invades Islam.*

CHAPTER 1

THE RAGING OF THE NATIONS

The word "rage" is particularly applicable at this point in time because the news media continues to reveal the rage of the Arab peoples. We point out, however, that the rage is not limited to the Arab nations, but includes the entire world.

The Rage of the Gentiles

"Why do the heathen rage, and the people imagine a vain thing? The kings of the earth set themselves, and the rulers take counsel together, against the LORD, and against his anointed, saying, Let us break their bands asunder, and cast away their cords from us" (Psalm 2:1-3).

The above Scripture reveals humanity's desire to be free of the "bands" and "cords," the God-ordained moral law for all of humanity at all times. These three verses summarize the whole earth—the heathen, the kings, and the rulers. That's the people, the political leaders and the intellectuals of the world. They all desire to do their own thing, to establish a world society so humanity can live together in peace and unity—that's their dream.

The Rage of the World

The statement that the world is in a rage may seem strange. The nations of the world collectively do not know the Lord or His Anointed. So, this must apply to the nation of Israel. But that causes a problem, because it plainly says "the heathen" and "the kings of the earth," so this is global. That means the whole world is in an uproar and in rebellion against the Lord and His Anointed.

> *The whole world is in an uproar and in rebellion against the Lord and His Anointed.*

The issue is democracy; in particular, how democracy is invading the whole world. This is not something that happened overnight, nor in the last few months or years, but an issue that concerns all of human history. We must keep in mind the bigger picture, the whole story of humanity; otherwise, we get stuck into little sidelines such as debating atheism, communism, socialism, capitalism, nationalism, and innumerable other "isms" that have developed throughout the 6,000 years of civilization.

But there is more: the motivating factor is revealed with the words, "against the Lord and against His anointed." That is the cause of division between the nations, races, and ethnic groups. And that is why Satan is working overtime to bring the Gentile world together, against the Anointed.

Jesus the Anointed

Bible readers are familiar with the story. Jesus of

Nazareth was recognized as a great teacher, healer, and prophet among the people of Israel. For about three and a half years, He walked across the Promised Land, demonstrating His messianic authority and proclaiming to the people, "The kingdom of heaven is at hand" (Matthew 4:17). Jesus had a great following; many recognized that He was sent from God.

When John the Baptist was cast into prison, he sent his disciples to Jesus with the question, "Art thou he that should come, or do we look for another?" (Matthew 11:3). Jesus answered: "The blind receive their sight, and the lame walk, the lepers are cleansed, and the deaf hear, the dead are raised up, and the poor have the gospel preached to them" (verse 5). Clearly, He manifested to Israel that He is the Son of God, the Messiah which was to come, the One Moses and all the prophets spoke of. That is one side of the story.

The Rage of Religion

The other side is the religious authority, symbolized by the glorious and beautiful temple on Mt. Moriah in Jerusalem. The priests, the scribes, the Pharisees and the Sadducees, although not in agreement with each other, had one thing in common: namely, that Jesus' teaching was contrary to their established tradition. They were faced with a dilemma—either reject Jesus as Israel's Messiah, or lose the Roman protective authority. This is evident from John 11:48: "If we let him thus alone, all men will believe on him: and the Romans shall come and take away both our place and nation."

Thus, only one option remained: get rid of Him.

Democratic Majority at Work

Jesus was arrested and brought before the Roman governor Pontius Pilate, who carefully examined Jesus but found no fault in Him. That was not according to the plan of the religious authorities; thus, we read, "But the chief priests and elders persuaded the multitude that they should ask Barabbas, and destroy Jesus" (Matthew 27:20). Here we see democracy in action. The multitude was guided by the chief priests and

> *This was democracy in action; thus, Jesus was executed, nailed to the cross, where He died that same day.*

elders to choose between Barabbas, a murderer, or Jesus. They chose Barabbas. To the question of what to do with Jesus, "They all say unto him, let him be crucified."

The masses of the people, the majority was in charge. This was democracy in action; thus, Jesus was executed, nailed to the cross, where He died that same day.

Who Was to Blame?

The crucifixion of Jesus took place in Jerusalem. During those days, there was no electronic communication, neither was there a printing press. The only possible communication was through letters, sending them via available mode of transportation.

Rome was the world power at that time. In order for the report of the crucifixion to reach Rome, it would take many weeks, if not months. The rest of the world knew nothing about the crucifixion of Jesus Christ in Jerusalem. Those are the apparent facts of this most important event in human history.

It is correct to state that this was a local issue between the religious authorities in Jerusalem, and

Jesus the loner who was deserted by all, even by His disciples. So we may rightly say that the outside world was not aware of the things that had transpired in Jerusalem. But that's not what the Bible says.

Sin Crucified Christ

Here is what we read in Acts 4:25-27: "Who by the mouth of thy servant David hast said, Why did the heathen rage, and the people imagine vain things? The kings of the earth stood up, and the rulers were gathered together against the Lord, and against his Christ. For of a truth against thy holy child Jesus, whom thou hast anointed, both Herod, and Pontius Pilate, with the Gentiles, and the people of Israel, were gathered together."

The words, "Why do the heathen rage?" include all people on the earth. In verse 26, "The kings of the earth" identifies all the leaders of the world. Herod, the king of Israel, Pontius Pilate, the official Roman governor, followed by the Gentiles.

The words, "Why do the heathen rage?" include all people on the earth.

That certainly means the whole world. Lastly, "the people of Israel." What did they do? They "were gathered together against the Lord, and against His Christ."

Let no one ever say that the crucifixion of Christ was a local matter. It was a global event. The consequences of this event reach into our days and will go beyond our time to the completion. This is documented in the last book of the Bible: "And he that sat upon the throne said, Behold, I make all things new" (Revelation 21:5).

It is of utmost importance to comprehend this tremendous truth, that when God deals with humanity, He includes all of history. When He allowed His Son to be nailed to the cross, where Jesus cried out dying, "It is finished," God the Father did precisely what He had proclaimed throughout history by His prophets. This is so powerfully summarized in one of the most popular verses in Holy Scripture, "For God so loved the world, that he gave his only begotten Son, that whosoever believeth in him should not perish, but have everlasting life" (John 3:16).

CHAPTER 2

RACING TOWARD GLOBAL DEMOCRACY

Virtually the entire world supports democracy because it gives power to the people. However, a grave danger is lurking around the corner; namely, the democratic invasion of the Church. Thus the question, to what extent will the Church be affected by democracy?

Historic Democracy

The introduction to the "History of democracy" by Wikipedia has this to say,

> The history of empowering people by giving them a say in their political entities—traces back to Athens to its re-emergence and rise from the 17th century to the present day. According to one definition, democracy is a political system in which all the members of the society have an equal share of formal political power. In modern representative democracy, this formal equality is embodied primarily in the right to vote.[1]

When reading the lengthy article, we realize that there are innumerable forms of democracy, but all have the same aim: power to the people, and power by the people.

While Greece is the originator of democracy, we should consider Rome as the practitioner. The Constitution of the Roman Republic emerged at around 500 B.C. There we find the Executive Magistrate Branch, the Senate and Legislative Assembly, definitions we are quite familiar with.

Under the section "Roman Republic" in that same article, Wikipedia introduces the subject:

> Even though Rome is classified as a Republic and not a democracy, its history has helped preserve the concept of

> democracy over the centuries. The Romans had great respect for classical Greek culture, and many Greek works... were preserved. Additionally, the Roman model of governance inspired many political thinkers over the centuries, and today's modern (representative) democracies imitate more the Roman than the Greek models.[2]

Webster's Dictionary defines the word "republic": "A state or nation in which the supreme power rests in all the citizens entitled to vote (the electorate) and is exercised by representatives elected, directly or indirectly, by them and responsible to them."[3] Under the word "democracy," we read, "Government in which the people hold the ruling power either directly or through elected representatives; rule by the ruled."[4] In both cases, it is the power by the people, for the people.

Resurrection of Democracy

The United States of America can be credited as the major contributing power initiating the resurrection of democracy in modern times.

The US was extremely successful in establishing a democratic union by unifying the various European nationalities into one identity—Americans.

America Built on Roman Example

Democracy did not originate in America, but Rome. The following quotation from *National Geographic*, August 1997, page 70 states:

> Impressed by the checks and balances of the Roman system, the authors of American government also made sure that an official who violated the law could be 'impeached,' a word we take from the Roman practice of putting wayward magistrates in pedica.
>
> 'The reliance on Roman structures at the birth of the United States was reflected in early American popular culture, which delighted in drawing parallels between U.S. leaders and the noble Romans.
>
> 'There was a great vogue for marble statues depicting George Washington, Alexander Hamilton, even Andrew Jackson in Roman attire. A larger-than-life statue of Washington in a toga and sandals is still on exhibit at the National Museum of American History in Washington, D.C.'[5]

At the beginning of this article in *National Geographic*, we read this on page 15:

> In the year 509 B.C. the patrician families of Rome set up a quasi-representative form of government, with a pair of ruling consuls elected for a one-year term. This marked the beginning of the Roman Republic, a form of government that would continue until Julius Caesar crossed the Rubicon 460

> years later. Those five centuries were marked by increasing prosperity and increasing democracy.[6]

Democracy Evolving

The assumption that democracy is set in stone, such as in the American Constitution, is far from the truth. Democracy continues to develop as days go by. Under the subtitle "Progressive Democracy," the following is from our book, *Satan's Last Victory*, pages 137-138:

> Although democracy was the driving force during the time of the Declaration of Independence in America, it was a very limited democracy. From the approximately four million people living in the country, only about 100,000 had the right to vote. In plain words, this right was reserved for the well-to-do landowners. Ironically, many of these landowners received the land from the Monarch of England, against whom they rebelled.
>
> Women, for example, were not allowed to vote until 1920. Blacks were not considered full human beings. When we keep these facts in mind, then the words we find in the Declaration of Independence sound rather hollow for those who did not have the right as citizens: 'We hold these truths to be self-evident, that all men are created equal, that they are endowed by the Creator with certain inalienable rights, that among these are life, liberty and the pursuit of happiness.'

> Today all that has changed. Democracy makes all people equal, but it was accomplished progressively, and we must add, this is not yet the end.[7]

> *Nobody wants authoritarian government or dictators; people want to be free to do their own thing.*

Democracy and Mankind

Democracy, as stated previously, represents people power. In general, that is to be welcomed. Nobody wants authoritarian government or dictators; people want to be free to do their own thing.

Now comes the problem: the Bible says all people are sinners, therefore evil and corrupt. "He that committeth sin is of the devil" is the blanket statement of Holy Scripture. Thus the question, can an evil society bring forth righteous judgment, true peace, and lasting prosperity? The answer is, impossible!

The Devil's Clever Devices

The devil is not stupid; he has plans, and he knows precisely what he wants. Here is his grand design: make all the people of the world participants of their desire, give all democracy, let the people be in charge and, most importantly, let the church join in.

> *The greatest danger is a false Christianity, because it will lead to eternal damnation.*

That is the greatest danger—not the Muslims, the communists, the atheists, the terrorists, etc. The greatest danger is a false Christianity, because it will lead to eternal damnation.

Church and State

Virtually all countries established by Europeans throughout the world, follow in the footsteps of the Vatican doctrine, which insists on the unity between government and the church, preferably with the church being in charge.

A fitting summary was written by Pope Leo XIII, and is found on the first page of the book, *The Great Encyclical Letters of Pope Leo XIII:* "...If society is to be healed now, in no other way can it be healed save by a return to Christian life and Christian institutions. When a society is perishing, the wholesome advice to give to those who would restore it is to recall it to the principles from which it sprang."[8]

The pages of this book are not to debate how the various nations of the world understand the function of religion and the government. The reader is encouraged to do his/her own research.

In the United States, the mixing of religion with politics is clearly expressed in the mottos, "One Nation Under God" and "In God We Trust." These slogans are engrained in the minds of the population. No one would ever dare suggest to take them out. However, that has caused the Church to become entangled in the global political democratic process.

A Voice from 1898

Here I will quote some more material from my book, *Revelation 13: Satan's Last Victory*, pages 121-124:

How democracy is developing and how it affects Christianity, was the subject Samuel J. Andrews wrote about in his book, *Christianity and Anti-Christianity in Their Final Conflict,* published by Moody Press, original copyright 1898. The following are a few excerpts:

> It is not to be questioned that social and political conditions have much influence in molding religious opinions, and we assume that the democratic spirit will rule the future. What kind of religious influence is Democracy adapted to exert? In what direction does the democratic current run? According to De Tocqueville, it runs in the direction of very general ideas, and therefore to Pantheism. The idea of the unity of the people as a whole, as one, preponderates, and this extends itself to the world, and to the universe. God and the universe make one whole. This unity has charms for men living in democracies, and prepares them for Pantheistic beliefs. "Among the different systems, by whose aid philosophy endeavors to explain the universe, I believe Pantheism to be one of those most fitted to seduce the human mind in democratic ages; and against it all who abide in their attachment to the true greatness of men, should struggle and combine."
>
> If these remarks of this very acute political observer are true, we may expect to see Pantheism enlarging its influence in Christendom as Democracy extends. (254-55)[9]

Samuel Andrews was not concerned so much about the political development but rather the effects on Christianity.

Under the chapter, "Antichrist as Head of the Nations," he writes:

> More and more all sovereigns and rulers are eager to learn what the wishes of their people are, and careful not to set themselves in direct opposition to them. Whether in the exist-

> ing monarchies hereditary succession will give place to popular election, is not certain, though it seems probable; but all rulers, hereditary or elected, are made more and more to feel themselves the servants of the people.
>
> This growth of Democracy serves to prepare the way of the Antichrist by making the popular will supreme, both as to the choice of the rulers and the nature and extent of their rule; and by giving legal expression to that will. When a people elects its legislators, the legislation will be what the majority of the voters demand. In the past, among all Christian nations, such legislation has, a great part, been based upon Christian principles, and involved the recognition of God's authority. So long as this authority, as declared in the Scriptures or by the Church, is recognized, the popular will is not supreme; but according as it is denied, this supremacy is more and more enlarged. If, then, the belief become general, either that there is no God, the Lawgiver, or no expression of His will which is authoritative, what principle shall determine the character and limitations of legislation? The only principle is that of the public good; whatever this demands, is right. If, for example, the law of marriage given in the Bible is set aside as without authority, what shall determine what the new law shall be? It must be what the welfare of society demands, and this is a matter of popular judgment. (264-65)[10]

Very plainly, what is good for the people and for the nation is going to become the final authority. The popular will of the people will become Law!

He then writes:

> We have reason to believe that, although the practical rejection of all now recognized Divine law may be gradual, the popular supremacy, based upon the public good, will at last be affirmed as absolute in all matters pertaining to man's welfare.
>
> As Democracy makes the popular will supreme, so it provides in general suffrage the legal means of its expression. It is possible that, as regards rulers, this may find its last and highest illustration in the choice between Christ and the Antichrist. As at the end of the Lord's earthly life the Jews were called upon, in a way which we must regard as providential (Matthew 27:15), to choose between Him and Barabbas; so again will He be presented before the covenant peoples—the Christian nations—not indeed as personally present, that they may choose between Him and the Lawless One. The choice of the Antichrist is not to be the choice of the rulers only, or of the popular leaders, the multitude being unwilling, and silent, and passive; it is the act of the peoples, the direct or indirect expression of the popular will. It is the voluntary declaration of Christendom. (266)[11]

Democracy has enveloped Churchianity to such an extent that it has become impossible to recognize a distinct difference between the world and the church. The popular will of the people is the law![12]

Democracy Invasion Continues

When we understand these truths, we recognize that the democracy invasion of the Arab world is all but natural. This has no relationship to the continual setbacks, neither the redirection of some dictatorships; the end will still be the same. All nations of the world will and must fulfill what we quoted at the beginning of chapter one: "Why do the heathen rage, and the people imagine a vain thing? The kings of the earth set themselves, and the rulers take counsel together, against the LORD, and against his anointed, saying, Let us break their bands asunder, and cast away their cords from us" (Psalm 2:1-3).

CHAPTER 3

SATAN'S INVISIBLE POWER ELITE

The guiding factor behind all the commotion in the world—the uprisings, revolutions, wars and rebellion—is the master deceiver, the enemy of God. He is also called the god of this world and the prince of darkness. At his disposal are innumerable fallen angels we call demons.

How the political world relates to the powers of darkness is revealed in this chapter.

The Prince of Darkness

Never must we allow ourselves to be distracted by the visible manifestation of politicians or world leaders, who seem to have a sway with the masses. Behind all of them stands the prince of darkness, the god of this world.

The primary issue we're dealing with in this book relates to democracy and the Arab world. We refuse to speculate on or identify certain political parties or movements responsible for the Arab uprising. The real power behind all these things belongs to the father of lies, the murderer from the beginning, the one identified in Revelation 12:9 and 20:2 as "...the dragon, that old serpent, which is the Devil, and Satan."

Never must we allow ourselves to be distracted by the visible manifestation of politicians or world leaders, who seem to have a sway with the masses. Behind all of them stands the prince of darkness, the god of this world.

The Persian Example

The prophet Daniel reveals some fascinating

truths about the invisible power elite in chapter 10:

"In the third year of Cyrus king of Persia a thing was revealed unto Daniel, whose name was called Belteshazzar; and the thing was true, but the time appointed was long: and he understood the thing, and had understanding of the vision. In those days I Daniel was mourning three full weeks. I ate no pleasant bread, neither came flesh nor wine in my mouth, neither did I anoint myself at all, till three whole weeks were fulfilled" (verses 1-3).

Something special was revealed to Daniel. What was it? In verse 14, the angel tells him: "Now I am come to make thee understand what shall befall thy people in the latter days...."

That means the prime reason for the angel to answer Daniel's prayer was to tell what would happen to the Jews "in the latter days." But in reading the book of Daniel, particularly the four visions he received, we find very little said about his people. The message concerns the entire world. But that fact makes us realize that all of world history turns around the Jew.

Daniel Believed in Prophecy

Why did Daniel pray and fast for three weeks? He

desired to find the answer from God regarding his people. Daniel prepares himself for the redemption of Israel from Babylonian captivity.

"In the first year of Darius the son of Ahasuerus, of the seed of the Medes, which was made king over the realm of the Chaldeans; In the first year of his reign I Daniel understood by books the number of the years, whereof the word of the LORD came to Jeremiah the prophet, that he would accomplish seventy years in the desolations of Jerusalem" (Daniel 9:1-2). He surely believed the prophecy written by Jeremiah. Although no sin of Daniel is mentioned, he nevertheless begins to confess the sins of Israel and his own. This is quite evident from the words, "we," "us," "ours" and "my." That's the main focus of chapter 9.

Prophetic Visions for the Endtimes

Then Daniel receives the answer: "At the beginning of thy supplications the commandment came forth, and I am come to shew thee; for thou art greatly beloved: therefore understand the matter, and consider the vision" (Daniel 9:23).

Strangely, Daniel does not get information regarding the release from Babylonian captivity, but rather the angel gives him a prophetic vision of the distant future—the coming of the Messiah, His dying, the destruction of Jerusalem, the long silence in Israel's history, followed by the return of the Jews to Israel, then the reestablishment of the covenant leading to the abomination of desolation and the rulership of Antichrist.

This vision reaches into our time and beyond. Antichrist indeed will establish peace for Israel and the entire world. Then later, he reveals himself as the great imposter whom Daniel identifies with these words, "And the king shall do according to his will; and he shall exalt himself, and magnify himself above every god, and shall speak marvellous things against the God of gods, and shall prosper till the indignation be accomplished: for that that is determined shall be done" (Daniel 11:36).

Prayer Answered

"Therefore I was left alone, and saw this great vision, and there remained no strength in me: for my comeliness was turned in me into corruption, and I retained no strength" (Daniel 10:8). Next, the unidentified heavenly host comforts him,

"...Fear not, Daniel: for from the first day that thou didst set thine heart to understand, and to chasten thyself before thy God, thy words were heard, and I am come for thy words" (verse 12).

Who Is This Prince of Persia?

From the very first day, Daniel's prayer came before God, yet there was something hindering the delivery: "But the prince of the kingdom of Persia withstood me one and twenty days: but, lo, Michael, one of the chief princes, came to help me; and I remained there with the kings of Persia" (Daniel 10:13). This is speaking of a heavenly host of darkness, in this case, the "Prince of Persia" and the "kings of Persia."

Daniel had no reason to be in conflict with the prince or the kings, because he was part of that government; thus, we know it speaks of the demonic angelic forces of Persia.

Apparently, the kingdom of darkness is well organized. They have "kings" and there is a "prince of the kingdom of Persia." These are the demonic powers that withstood the angelic host sent to bring the prophetic message to Daniel the Jew.

Realizing that the devil had his prince and kings that were in charge of Persia, we must come to the conclusion that such is the case with all nations of the world. Not surprisingly, the devil is called the god of this world.

The Multitude of Fallen Angels

We have no idea as to the number of these demonic forces, except for the fact that the Bible states one-third of the angelic host sided with Lucifer; thus, we may assume they were innumerable.

Let's see a New Testament example. Mark 5 reports of "an unclean spirit." Verses 6-7 reveal the dialogue: "But when he saw Jesus afar off, he ran and worshipped him, and cried with a loud voice, and said, What have I to do with thee, Jesus, thou Son of the most high God? I adjure thee by God, that thou torment me not." Jesus then asks him a question, "What is thy name?" Next comes an interesting revelation, "My name is Legion: for we are many" (verse 9).

If one were to assume a Roman legion, then it could be as many as 6,000. When we consider such possibilities, realizing that hundreds of millions of people may be possessed, then we may be talking about numbers the world could not contain.

The Invisible Enemy

This fact reinforces the Bible's claim that we as Christians should not be involved in the things revealed in the visible world, with its manifestation of evil. Our enemies are "principalities...powers...rulers of darkness...spiritual wickedness in high places" (Ephesians 6:12), not political leaders or governments.

The invisible powers are at work; not just in the Arab world right now, but they have been at work throughout history and will be in the future until Jesus makes an end of all opposing powers.

Another Example, King Tyrus

To make sure that this is understood in proper context, let us look at another figure in the Bible, the King of Tyrus. We plainly read in Ezekiel 28:12, "Son of man, take up a lamentation upon the king of Tyrus, and say unto him...." Tyrus is a historical city, geographically identifiable; it is located to the north of Israel. But when we continue to read the lamentation, we notice that this speaks about a much greater power than the human King of Tyrus.

For example, "Thou sealest up the sum, full of wisdom, and perfect in beauty." Can that be said of the earthly King of Tyrus? Absolutely not.

The next verse makes it even clearer, "Thou hast been in Eden the garden of God...." This prophecy goes back to the very beginning, when God created man in His own image and placed him in the garden of Eden. That's definitely not the earthly King Tyrus.

Furthermore, "Thou art the anointed cherub." Plainly, a heavenly identity, not to be compared with an earthly person.

Finally, Ezekiel 28:15 declares: "Thou wast perfect in thy ways from the day that thou wast created, till iniquity was found in thee." No man on earth was perfect except Adam when he was created and the Son of Man, Jesus Christ, who was without sin.

Thus we see, prophecies are visions from heaven, identifying activity on earth driven by the powers of darkness.

Did Peter Become Satan?

One more example: when Jesus asked His disciples, "But whom say ye that I am?" we read, "Simon Peter answered and said, Thou art the Christ, the Son of the living God" (Matthew 16:15-16). Take note of Jesus' reply, "Blessed art thou, Simon Barjona: for flesh and blood hath not revealed it unto thee, but my Father which is in heaven" (verse 17). Jesus identified the words Peter spoke as revelation given from the Father in heaven. Peter himself did not come up with the statement, "Thou art the Christ, the Son of the living God."

A little later, when Jesus predicted that He would suffer many things and be killed, Peter said, "Be it far from thee, Lord: this shall not be unto thee" (verse 22). How did Jesus answer this time? "But he turned, and said unto Peter, Get thee behind me, Satan: thou art an offence unto me: for thou savourest not the things that be of God, but those that be of men" (verse 23). This is directly addressed unto Peter, "Get thee behind me, Satan." Does that mean Peter became Satan? No, but the words Peter spoke were by the inspiration of Satan.

These few examples should show that "the prince of the kingdom of Persia" and "the kings of

Persia" are not physical, earthly identities but demonic powers: they are Satan's invisible power elite.

Prophecy Neglected

It is not surprising that Satan does everything in his power to hinder the teaching of the prophetic Word in most churches.

Now we should understand why the prophetic Word is neglected in many churches. The Bible is a prophetic book, "…the testimony of Jesus is the spirit of prophecy" (Revelation 19:10). Only Holy Scripture gives us the beginning and the end and everything that is in between. We are admonished to read the prophetic Word and to listen to it: "Blessed is he that readeth, and they that hear the words of this prophecy, and keep those things which are written therein: for the time is at hand" (Revelation 1:3).

It is not surprising that Satan does everything in his power to hinder the teaching of the prophetic Word in most churches. The proclamation of prophecy must be precluded at any cost. That is Satan's aim.

This is also evident from the event recorded in Matthew 8, when Jesus met two people possessed with demons. We read in verse 29: "And, behold, they cried out, saying, What have we to do with thee, Jesus, thou Son of God? art thou come hither to torment us before the time?" Not only did the demons know that it was Jesus the Son of God, but they also knew that this was "before the time." They apparently knew that Jesus would come, destroy the work of the devil, establish the Church of Jesus Christ on earth, then cast the devil and his angels into the lake of fire, the ultimate destination of the powers of darkness. Bible prophecy is indeed a direct confrontation of Satan's plan. Thus, he attempts to silence the prophetic Word.

Prophecy Alive Today

Many Christians make the mistake of separating the Word of God as the Old Testament, the Law, the Gospel, and prophecy. Usually, prophecy is defined with the Latin word "eschatology," which means to deal with the future. If Bible prophecy only deals with the future, then justifiably, we can put it aside, but prophecy is just as active and just as important today as it was 2,000 years ago when the Church was founded.

The Apostle Paul makes this statement in Ephesians 2:20: "And are built upon the foundation of the apostles and prophets, Jesus Christ himself being the chief corner stone." The apostles represent the New Testament, the prophets the Old Testament, and those are built upon the cornerstone, Jesus Christ.

We love our country, respect and honor our government, but should never change the truth of the Word of God, which clearly states, "The whole world lieth in wickedness."

The point I wish to make by quoting these Bible references is for us to realize that we are in a battle against the invisible world, the powers of darkness, the god of this world, and therefore cannot afford to ignore prophetic Scripture.

Where Is the Evil Empire?

Do not permit yourself to be led astray by Republicans, Democrats, liberals, or conservatives; none of them can do anything that would change the prophetic Word.

We love our country, respect and honor our government, but should never change the truth of the Word of God, which clearly states, "The whole world lieth in wickedness." Jesus Christ gave Himself, "...that he might deliver us from this present evil world, according to the will of God and our Father" (Galatians 1:4). That, my friend, is the bottom line.

When we take the Word of God seriously, we suddenly recognize with horror what an insult it is to Jesus Christ our Lord when we proclaim nationalistic slogans, "We are the greatest...we are the freest...we love peace...we are righteous, etc." Such slogans are inspired by the father of lies, Satan. When it comes to the nations of the world, Isaiah has this to say: "All nations before him are as nothing; and they are counted to him less than nothing, and vanity" (Isaiah 40:17).

Satan's Global World

Understanding the spiritual background of these developments, we immediately realize that the devil is at work today, as he always has been since the Garden of Eden. He is now in the process of creating a truly global world where all the nations can live in peace and harmony with one another, where prosperity abounds, and where the people of the world are being made rich through political, financial, and economic fornication.

Many excellent Bible scholars desperately try to warn us that the Muslims are taking over the world. But it won't happen. Why not? There is no room in Holy Scripture to support the theory of a Muslim invasion of Europe and the rest of the world.

We are fully aware that the pages of this book contradict a majority of Christian teachers. Many excellent Bible scholars desperately try to warn us that the Muslims are taking over the world. But it won't happen. Why not? There is no room in Holy Scripture to support the theory of a Muslim invasion of Europe and the rest of the world.

Prophecy clearly identifies only four Gentile superpowers, the first being Babylon, the second Medo-Persia, the third Greece, and the last one Rome. The Roman power structure continues until this very day. The fundamental principles of law and government, of citizenship and civil responsibility throughout the world are based upon Roman laws.

The visible part of Satan's power elite are the governments on earth. But behind each government, there are innumerable demons that take their orders from Satan's invisible power elite. That, however, does not mean the government is our enemy; on the contrary, we are urged to obey our government as instructed in Roman 13.

To conclude this chapter, we summarize what we have learned: behind the present Arab Revolution stands a demonic power elite that will cause the Muslim world to be integrated into the global family of democratic nations, in order to establish the last great end-time world society under Antichrist.

CHAPTER 4

DEMOCRACY AND THE BIBLE

Many of us think that democracy, the power of the people, is something new and modern. Such is not the case; the Bible clearly reveals democracy in action during biblical times.

Every country on the face of the earth wants to be the greatest, wants to make themselves a name. Man has not changed; his heart is still hardened against God and filled with rebellion against the Holy One.

The Power of the People

Democracy is people power. What the people want, they eventually get. The Bible reports how the people were a decisive power when it came to decision making. Let us look at three examples: 1. the Tower of Babel; 2. Israel's rebellion; and 3. the crucifixion of our Lord.

1. Tower of Babel Democracy

In Genesis chapter 11, we read of the first democratic rebellion against God:

"And the whole earth was of one language, and of one speech. And it came to pass, as they journeyed from the east, that they found a plain in the land of Shinar; and they dwelt there. And they said one to another, Go to, let us make brick, and burn them thoroughly. And they had brick for stone, and slime had they for morter. And they said, Go to, let us build us a city and a tower, whose top may reach unto heaven; and let us make us a name, lest we be scattered abroad upon the face of the whole earth" (verses 1-4).

Interestingly, no king, no key person, strong leader, or some type of dictator is mentioned. But the words "they," "us" and "we" clearly demonstrate the will of "we the people." They did things their way, "let us make us a name." That's what every nation has attempted to do since the days of the Tower of Babel. Every country on the face of the earth wants to be the greatest, wants to make themselves a name. Man has not changed; his heart is still hardened against God and filled with rebellion against the Holy One.

National Pride Barometer

The National Opinion Research Center (NORC) in Chicago, Illinois, lists the top ten nations that answered positively to the question, "My country is better than most in the world." Five points indicated the maximum.[13]

Japan	4.3
USA	4.2
Bulgaria	4.1
New Zealand	4.1

Canada	4.1
Austria	4.0
Russia	4.0
Ireland	3.8
Norway	3.8
Poland	3.7

2. Israel's Democratic Rebellion

The power of the people was also evident in the nation of Israel. After being led out by the Lord from the slavery of Egypt, it didn't take long before "people power" became apparent: "And the people murmured against Moses, saying, What shall we drink?" (Exodus 15:24). From that point on, over and again the nation of Israel tried to do their own thing, attempting to cast off the rulership of the Lord, the God of heaven and earth, and replace it with people power.

After they had entered the Promised Land, judges ruled the nation, but several centuries later, we read of a democratic rebellion against the God of Israel in 1 Samuel 8:4-5: "Then all the elders of Israel gathered themselves together, and came to Samuel unto Ramah, And said unto him, Behold, thou art old, and thy sons walk not in thy ways:

now make us a king to judge us like all the nations." In spite of Samuel's insistence that Israel is making a bad choice, verses 19-20 say: "Nevertheless the people refused to obey the voice of Samuel; and they said, Nay; but we will have a king over us; That we also may be like all the nations; and that our king may judge us, and go out before us, and fight our battles."

3. Democracy and the Crucifixion

When Jesus was arrested and led before Pontius Pilate the governor, we see democracy in action: "...Pilate said unto them, Whom will ye that I release unto you? Barabbas, or Jesus which is called Christ?" (Matthew 27:17). They chose Barabbas. Why? "...The chief priests and elders persuaded the multitude that they should ask Barabbas, and destroy Jesus" (verse 20). The crowd assembled, became anti-Jesus, and was able to persuade the Roman authority to do its will: "Pilate saith unto them, What shall I do then with Jesus which is called Christ? They all say unto him, Let him be crucified" (verse 22). People power had the upper hand, "And Pilate gave sentence that it should be as they required" (Luke 23:24).

Also, the Acts of the Apostles reports that the crucifixion of the Son of God was initiated by the whole world: "The kings of the earth stood up, and the rulers were gathered together against the Lord, and against his Christ. For of a truth against thy holy child Jesus, whom thou hast anointed, both Herod, and Pontius Pilate, with the Gentiles, and the people of Israel, were gathered together" (Acts 4:26-27). Of course, "the kings of the earth" had no idea what was happening in Jerusalem, neither the "Gentiles." The only ones directly involved were King Herod, Pontius Pilate, and the Jews in Jerusalem, but from spiritual perspectives, all are included—the rulers on earth, with the Gentiles and Israel as well. Why? Because ALL have sinned, all are sinners, and Jesus died for all sinners.

CHAPTER 5

THE JEWS, THE CHURCH AND THE GENTILES

In this chapter, we will explain how the persecution of the Jews and the Church relates to the establishment of Israel and the demise of the Soviet Union. We will also reveal how the devil is using imagined enemies to detract the Church from its Great Commission.

The Best and the Worst to Come

Before we occupy ourselves with this chapter, "The Jews, the Church and the Gentiles," let us first read the following words from Revelation 12:12: "Therefore rejoice, ye heavens, and ye that dwell in them. Woe to the inhabiters of the earth and of the sea! for the devil is come down unto you, having great wrath, because he knoweth that he hath but a short time." This Scripture distinguishes two categories of people in two different locations: those in heaven and those on earth. The first shall rejoice; the last will experience the great wrath. In brief, that is the finality of humanity.

Silencing the Church and the Jews

While the Church is still on earth, Satan, the great deceiver, the murderer from the beginning, the father of lies, tries desperately to destroy or at least silence the Church of Jesus Christ and the people of Israel.

From Scripture as well as other historic writings, we know that the Jews experienced severe persecution. Volumes of literature testify to that fact. Who is to blame? Everybody. Why? Because it is the fruit of sin. The Bible says, "All have sinned," and, "He who sins is of the devil." That is the plain truth.

Israel's Fall Foretold

Moses foretold Israel's horrible future, "And the LORD shall scatter thee among all people, from the one end of the earth even unto the other; and there thou shalt serve other gods, which neither thou nor thy fathers have known, even wood and stone. And among these nations shalt thou find no ease, neither shall the sole of thy foot have rest: but the LORD shall give thee there a trembling heart, and failing of eyes, and sorrow of mind: And thy life shall hang in doubt before thee; and thou shalt fear day and night, and shalt have none assurance of thy life" (Deuteronomy 28:64-66). That is precisely what happened; Israel fell for the devil's deception.

Why Gentiles Hate Israel

If we ask why such severe persecution, we find two answers in Scripture: 1) Israel continued to rebel against the living God; subsequently, they were cast out of their land and lived among the nations of the world for over 2,000 years. 2) Satan, through the hands of the Gentile world, tries desperately to destroy the Jewish people. The reason is Jesus' statement, "Salvation is of the Jews." The devil hates salvation; therefore, he vehemently opposes Israel.

An Escape for Israel

Revelation 12:13-14 reads: "And when the dragon saw that he was cast unto the earth, he persecuted the woman which brought forth the man child. And to the woman were given two wings of a great eagle, that she might fly into the wilderness, into her place, where she is nourished for a time, and times, and half a time, from the face of the serpent." Who is this woman? It is Israel, the Jewish people.

For clarity's sake, let us also read verses 1, 2 and 5: "And there appeared a great wonder in heaven; a woman clothed with the sun, and the moon under her feet, and upon her head a crown of twelve stars: And she being with child cried, travailing in birth, and pained to be delivered...And she brought forth a man child, who was to rule all nations with a rod of iron: and her child was caught up unto God, and to his throne." Scholars agree this speaks of Jesus of Nazareth, the King of the Jews.

That's the good news; there is an escape prepared for the Jewish people: "And the woman fled into the wilderness, where she hath a place prepared of God, that they should feed her there a thousand two hundred and threescore days" (Revelation 12:6).

The Church Also Persecuted

The Church too suffered persecution right from the beginning. We see this documented in Acts 8:1: "And Saul was consenting unto his death. And at that time there was a great persecution against the church which was at Jerusalem; and they were all scattered abroad throughout the regions of Judaea and Samaria, except the apostles."

In chapter 11 verse 19, we read again: "Now they which were scattered abroad upon the persecution that arose about Stephen traveled as far as Phenice, and Cyprus, and Antioch, preaching the word to none but unto the Jews only."

Later in Romans 8:35, we have this statement, "Who shall separate us from the love of Christ? shall tribulation, or distress, or persecution, or famine, or nakedness, or peril, or sword?"

In 2 Timothy 3:12, we read, "Yea, and all that will live godly in Christ Jesus shall suffer persecution." The Apostle Paul makes it abundantly clear that suffering, persecution and tribulation are part of the life experience of a true believer in Jesus Christ. The reason? "...knowing that tribulation worketh patience" (Romans 5:3).

In the World But Not of the World

The Church is not a country or a nation; she is global and does not belong to any of the 192 UN recognized nations on planet Earth.[14] The Church resides among the nations for a specific purpose: to be light and salt.

It stands to reason, therefore, that Satan—the enemy of our souls—tries desperately to silence the testimony of the Church, and he does so through deception.

In reading 2 Corinthians 11:4, we notice how the enemy works: "For if he that cometh preacheth another Jesus, whom we have not preached, or if ye receive another spirit, which ye have not received, or another gospel, which ye have not accepted, ye might well bear with him." Therefore, another Jesus, another spirit, and another gospel is the real enemy in the Church.

Endtime Danger of False Alarms

Unfortunately, the devil is rather successful in penetrating the Church with his false teachings. One of the cleverest tactics he uses in our days is sensationalism and the alarm about the Muslim danger. The devil likes to divert the attention of the Church away from the Great Commission to preach the Gospel to all nations. He wants us to focus our attention and resources on something else—in this case, Islam. Christian publications, books, radio and TV programs have lately been fixated on the danger of Islam, ignoring the words of Jesus that even the devil will not prevail against His Church.

The devil likes to divert the attention of the Church away from the Great Commission to preach the Gospel to all nations. He wants us to focus our attention and resources on something else—in this case, Islam.

"Fighting Communism"

Those of us who are old enough remember how the Church, particularly in the USA, fought Soviet communism with all means available. We were told that communism is the Church's enemy.

While residing in the city of Hamilton, Ohio in the late sixties, I went down a couple of blocks to the local cemetery and watched a number of memorial services, some conducted by churches, others by the military. In one corner I noticed a group of men whom I thought had peculiar garments on. Being inquisitive, I approached one of those men and asked the question: "What is this all about?" He replied, "We are fighting communism." "What is your means of accomplishing this fight?" I asked. Somewhat perplexed, he answered, "Well, we talk about it." That was a representative of the Ku Klux Klan.

I am definitely not a friend of communism, because I have some experience with East German communism, and it was the cause of me being a refugee. Also, I was once arrested and detained for unauthorized travel in the GDR (German Democratic Republic), so I am familiar with the system. But despite this, it was quite a surprise to hear and read the extreme anti-communist campaigns within Churchianity by the overwhelming majority who had absolutely no idea what communism actually was.

Our Real Enemy

Speaking of enemies, they are clearly listed in Holy Scripture, such as Galatians 5:17, "For the flesh lusteth against the Spirit, and the Spirit against the flesh: and these are contrary the one to the other: so that ye cannot do the things that ye would." That brings the fight right into home territory, which we do not like. We would rather fight against an imagined enemy.

The Fall of Soviet Communism

In the end, however, we saw Soviet communism collapse in itself after 70 years. What was the cause? There are many reasons for the demise of this system, but let us mention two:

1. The prosperity of West Germany. Under the leadership of socialist Willy Brandt, Chancellor of Germany, the doors to the East were opened under the *Ostpolitik*, allowing communist East Germany to receive almost unlimited aid from the West.

Billions were paid for the release of so-called political prisoners. This moneymaking mechanism for the communist required the opening of *Intershops*, where people could buy merchandise, but only with hard currency such as the Deutsche Mark. With those doors open, products came into East Germany and other parts of the Soviet dominated bloc, clearly demonstrating that the goods of the West were superior. That was the first seed of discontent sown in the minds of East German citizens, which finally exploded in unprecedented protest marches in major cities and forced the East German government to open access to the West, 9 November 1989.

Soviet Communism and Jews

2. The other reason for the demise of the Soviet Union was the return of the Jewish people to the land of Israel. The overwhelming majority of Israelis have their roots in the Soviet Union.

Prophecy had to be fulfilled, such as Jeremiah 23:7-8: "Therefore, behold, the days come, saith the LORD, that they shall no more say, The LORD liveth, which brought up the children of Israel out of the land of Egypt; But, The LORD

liveth, which brought up and which led the seed of the house of Israel out of the north country, and from all countries whither I had driven them; and they shall dwell in their own land." The Jews had to come from "the north country," that is, Russia.

The Jewish immigrant's close and friendly relationship with the communist Soviet Union can be clearly seen in the official symbol of the Mapai Party. It prominently displayed the hammer and sickle, revealing its connection with the Labor and Socialist International.[15]

During Israel's first election in 1949, the Mapai won 35.7 percent of the vote, well ahead of the second placed Mapam Party with 14.7 percent.[16]

Not surprisingly, the Soviet Union was first to recognize the newly proclaimed State of Israel. Only the USSR delivered weapons to Israel, while the UK and the US had an arms embargo for the Middle East.

However, that friendship did not last long. A few years later, Russian Jews did not receive exit visas to migrate to Israel. That, however, caused even more desire in the hearts of the Jews in the Soviet Union to return to Israel, and return they did. We must accept this as the greatest reason for the existence and demise of the Soviet Union.

Evolution Battle

In recent times, the great battle within Churchianity has been against evolution. Obviously, evolution and atheistic communism go hand in hand. But does it really relate to the true Church? That should always be our question. Proclaiming the Gospel will always defeat any enemy.

Who is our enemy? Here, we must read 2 Timothy 3:1-5, "This know also, that in the last days perilous times shall come. For men shall be lovers of their own selves, covetous, boasters, proud, blasphemers, disobedient to parents, unthankful, unholy, without natural affection, trucebreakers, false accusers, incontinent, fierce, despisers of those that are good, traitors, heady, highminded, lovers of pleasures more than lovers of God; having a form of godliness, but denying the power thereof: from such turn away." These words are not addressed to the world, but to the Church. This is evident from the definition of the people, "...having a form of godliness."

War on Terror and Global Unity

Since the 11 September 2001 attack by Muslim terrorists in New York and Washington, the world's attention has been focused on terrorist activity, demonstrated by the much-publicized global war on terror.

Internationally, the media presented diverse opinions regarding the effectiveness of this global war against terrorism. While one may debate the pros and cons of the wars in Iraq and Afghanistan, one thing remains clear: united action to prevent terrorism is contributing progressively toward unity among the nations. When it comes to international travel, security measures are more stringent and harmonized than ever before. That's not really fighting terrorism, but forcing all nations into closer cooperation with one another.

CHAPTER 6

THE LAST SUPERPOWER

Scripture records four Gentile superpowers, the last one being Rome. Biblical facts invalidate the assumption of a fifth power, for example, Islam. Rome's (Europe's) dominion of the world is documented in this chapter.

Will Muslims Dominate the World?

Readers continue to send me various articles attempting to show the coming Muslim invasion of the West, particularly in Europe. Some reports almost convincingly show that Muslims will dominate Europe in the not-too-distant future.

We have received articles with titles such as, "Here Come the Muslims...American as the Last Man Standing...The Final Invasion of Europe...Muslim Dominion Planned...When Islam Becomes Law," etc., all pointing with conviction to the idea that Muslims will control Europe, and from there the rest of the world.

Rome or Islam?

What is our position regarding these theories? First, we must realize that the Bible provides for the existence of only four Gentile superpowers, namely 1. Babylon, 2. Persia, 3. Greece, and 4. Rome. Thus, no Muslim world superpower.

The Roman Empire is the longest lasting and, according to Scripture, incorporates the qualities, philosophy and religion of the previous three world empires.

All, however, will be displaced and destroyed by

the final world empire, the Kingdom of Peace, which the Lord Jesus Christ will set up in Israel, and from there rule the world.

A summary of the end of all nations is recorded in Daniel 2:44: "And in the days of these kings shall the God of heaven set up a kingdom, which shall never be destroyed: and the kingdom shall not be left to other people, but it shall break in pieces and consume all these kingdoms, and it shall stand for ever."

This simple fact demolishes any theories about world domination by Muslims, communists, atheists, or as the old slogan says, "the yellow peril." They all come and they all go.

The World's Final Superpower

Granted, Rome today cannot be recognized as a world superpower. It's only the capital city of Italy and world headquarters of the Roman Catholic Church. The media defined the former Soviet Union and the USA as superpowers. Right now, China is developing into the next superpower. But such definitions are temporary and shortsighted. For one thing, the Bible makes no provision for other Gentile superpowers, only the four we have listed. To define any other nation as a superpower will lead away from Scripture into confusion and speculation.

Roman World Dominion

Let us analyze Rome from historical and biblical perspectives, over the span of the last 2,000 years.

When Rome is mentioned, it is not limited to the city in Italy. Rome is much more. Historical records confirm that virtually all European nations attained their highest glory when they came under the protection of the Roman Empire.

Roman laws are the foundation upon which the world's civilized laws are established. Although Greece claims to be the originator of democracy, it was the Roman government that implemented a degree of democracy almost 2,500 years ago. Even a relatively modern country like the USA is based on Roman principles. Actually, the Roman Republic (509-49 BC) was the model for the Founding Fathers of the United States.

> The Roman process of making laws also had a deep influence on the American system. During the era of the Roman Republic (509 to 49 B.C.) lawmaking was a bicameral activity. Legislation was first passed by the comitia, the

> assembly of the citizens, then approved by the representative of the upper class, the senate, and issued in the name of the senate and the people of Rome. Centuries later, when the American Founding Fathers launched their bold experiment in democratic government, they took republican Rome as their model. Our laws, too, must go through two legislative bodies. The House of Representatives is our assembly of citizens, and, like its counterpart in ancient Rome, the U.S. Senate was originally designed as a chamber for the elite (it was not until the 17th Amendment, in 1913, that ordinary people were allowed to vote for their senators).
>
> (quoted in *Saddam's Mystery Babylon,* pages 31-32)[17]

The Global Power of Rome

In several of our articles and books, we have emphasized that the navies of the European colonial masters sailed the oceans of the world and subdued the nations and continents. Only Europe had the knowledge and power to conquer the world.

The prophet Daniel records the history of the times of the Gentiles, beginning with King Nebuchadnezzar of Babylon, and ending with a diverse looking monster as the last kingdom of the Gentiles.

That is fact, and nothing needs to be added.

Biblical Definition of Rome

Let us list some of the biblical descriptions of the fourth and final Gentile empire:

"And the fourth kingdom shall be strong as iron: forasmuch as iron breaketh in pieces and subdueth all things: and as iron that breaketh all these, shall it break in pieces and bruise. And whereas thou sawest the feet and toes, part of potters' clay, and part of iron, the kingdom shall be divided; but there shall be in it of the strength of the iron, forasmuch as thou sawest the iron mixed with miry clay. And as the toes of the feet were part of iron, and part of clay, so the kingdom shall be partly strong, and partly broken. And whereas thou sawest iron mixed with miry clay, they shall mingle themselves with the seed of men: but they shall not cleave one to another, even as iron is not mixed with clay" (Daniel 2:40-43).

In chapter 7, Daniel receives the first vision and describes the fourth beast in verse 7: "After this I saw in the night visions, and behold a fourth beast, dreadful and terrible, and strong exceedingly; and it had great iron teeth: it devoured and brake in pieces, and stamped the residue with the feet of it: and it was diverse from all the beasts that were before it; and it had ten horns."

Then he is told that, "These great beasts, which are four, are four kings, which shall arise out of the earth" (Daniel 7:17). It is unmistakable that this is global.

In verse 19, Daniel expresses his surprise and asks the question: "Then I would know the truth of the fourth beast, which was diverse from all the others, exceeding dreadful, whose teeth were of iron, and his nails of brass; which devoured, brake in pieces, and stamped the residue with his feet."

The answer is given in verse 23: "Thus he said, The fourth beast shall be the fourth kingdom upon earth, which shall be diverse from all kingdoms, and shall devour the whole earth, and shall tread it down, and break it in pieces."

These words are unmistakably clear: the last kingdom is diverse from all previous kingdoms. We are immediately reminded of the European Union's motto, "United in Diversity." Yet, this is not limited to Europe, but includes the whole earth, as we will see in a moment.

To understand the European influence and how this fourth kingdom "shall devour the whole earth," let us take a quick journey of the world's five continents.

The Americas

Here are some facts to consider: to the west of Europe lies the American continent (North and South). Thirty-five nations have been established in the so-called New World. I say "so-called," because there is no such thing as a "new world"; it is still the same old world created some 6,000 years ago. All 35 nations established on the American continent are based on Roman-European principles and laws; all speak European languages, and all have their roots in Europe.

Africa

Looking south from Europe, we find Africa. Again, virtually all of the 53 nations (more or less) were established or influenced by European colonial powers. Most of these nations can only communicate with one another by using European languages. Virtually all are founded upon the principles of Roman law. Much of Africa depends on aid and technology from Europe. Today, Europe is by far the largest contributor of foreign aid to the underdeveloped world.

Asia

To the east of Europe lies Asia. Most of that continent was at one time or another subdued by European colonial powers. The current conflict in Afghanistan is a clear example of former European dominion. Even Alexander the Great invaded the territory of today's Afghanistan.

Australia

The continent of Australia is member of the British Commonwealth. As late as the 1960s, immigration was limited to Europeans. Only a small number of people from Asia or Africa were accepted into the nation.

In summary, European influence and dominance of the world's five continents is demonstrably evident in modern history.

The Power of Diversity

How did this relatively small continent conquer the whole world? The answer is found in the diversity of the European nations. Each country developed its own language, culture, and custom to such an extent that one could not communicate with another. This diversity also led to fierce competition. When the Spanish, Portuguese, French, English, Dutch and others sailed the oceans, they did not cooperate, but clashed with one another. Innumerable wars between these European powers were the result. Because of this heated rivalry, Europe became fertile soil for new inventions and science, primarily for the purpose of destroying the competition; thus, the Industrial Revolution was born.

Bearing these facts in mind, virtually all theories regarding world dominion fall by the wayside. Only Europe qualifies as the candidate who "shall devour the whole earth, and shall tread it down, and break it in pieces."

"Devour...Tread Down...Break"

This may call for an explanation. What does it mean to devour, tread down, and break in pieces? It certainly sounds very negative, to say the least, and extremely destructive. But we must remember this is God's view of planet Earth, and not vice versa. What we think to be good does not necessarily mean God thinks likewise.

When it comes to "devour," I think we must allow for the possibility that it is democracy.

Indeed, democracy is "devouring" planet Earth. "Tread it down" means to force the nations to be subject to this new world order. And "break in pieces" certainly includes many of those cultures and traditions that were destroyed.

But most importantly, it is the changing of fundamental biblical laws into modern "free thinking." One item needs to be mentioned: God-ordained marriage. That is now being changed to cohabitation, and even Sodomites are entering the bonds of "marriage."

It is very helpful to analyze what God thinks of our society, not how we measure success and happiness. Not without reason, God declares, "For my thoughts are not your thoughts, neither are your ways my ways, saith the LORD" (Isaiah 55:8).

How does this all relate to the title of our book, *Democracy Invades Islam*? Read the next chapter.

(For more detailed information on Daniel's visions, see my book *Daniel's Prophecies Made Easy*.)

CHAPTER 7

THE MUSLIM'S LOSING BATTLE

The pro-democracy movement throughout the Arab world is a clear demonstration that Arabs were left out. They first missed the Industrial Revolution, then the technological and scientific explosion which caused the European world (West) to be prosperous.

Muslims Left Out

After the 13th century, while Europe's intellectual capacity was developing, the Muslim world remained stagnant. The only importance they attained was due to natural resources, primarily oil, which Europe and other industrialized nations needed.

> *To invade, dominate and rule other people, a high level of collective intelligence of the invading nation is required.*

Although many Arab countries have accumulated immense riches, the population at large is not benefiting. Besides the much needed and desired oil, there is little else coming from the Muslim world. The word poverty can be used to describe the bulk of these countries. Prosperity only exists for the few and the rich. True democracy resulting in political freedom for the people is only a dream. The intellectual capacity of the Arab Muslim world is virtually nonexistent when compared with the European world. This is evident when one looks at the Nobel Prize recipients.

The Nobel Prize has been awarded 829 times since first being awarded in 1901. Many Western countries have accumulated over 20 (and several over 100) recipients each, but the list from predominately Muslim countries is comparatively paltry.

Nobel Prize Winners from Predominately Muslim Nations[18]

Algeria	2
Bangladesh	1
Egypt	4
Iran	2
Pakistan	1
Palestine	1 (Yasser Arafat)

To invade, dominate and rule other people, a high level of collective intelligence of the invading nation is required. This is historically proven by the superior level of knowledge and technology of the former three Gentile superpowers: Babylon, Persia and Greece.

Brute Force of Non-Intellectuals

The lack of intelligence was particularly evident

during the 11th September 2001 (9/11) terrorist attack. If these religious fanatics would have had the intellectual capacity to cause the sophisticated computer system at the Pentagon to go haywire, causing the release of weapons of mass destruction or the destruction of internal secret government documents, then one would have to admit, these people are really dangerous. They would indeed be capable of destroying the United States, or for that matter, Europe as well. But no special intelligence was needed. These suicide terrorists, mostly from America's friend Saudi Arabia, literally used Stone Age methods to accomplish their murderous feat: knives (box cutters)! There is nothing more primitive than taking a knife and threatening or killing a person.

Granted, some of them trained as pilots. However, their sloppy planning which nevertheless succeeded pointed to the negligence of American intelligence agencies. Furthermore, subsequent terrorist attacks and attempts show that these 20 hijackers were by far the best that militant Islam had to offer.

Money Matters

Money, as we all know, rules the world. Wilfred

Hahn documents in *Eternal Value Review* the following: "60% of the world's wealth is dominated by historically Christian countries, which make up only 10% of the world's population. Christendom, based on Roman principles, is dominating planet Earth."[19]

Hahn further reveals that the average annual income in predominantly Muslim countries is $1,145, while the 45 high-income historically Christian countries earn $27,033. In the financial world, Muslim nations barely account for 1% of the value of world equity markets.

In the meantime, some progress is to be noted. Forbes.com reports the following under "Islamic Finance":

> Islamic Finance is Booming. At least $500 billion in assets around the world are managed in accordance with Sharia, or Islamic law, and the sector is growing at more than 10% per year. In spirit, Islamic finance seeks to promote social justice by banning exploitative practices. In reality, this boils down to a set of prohibitions—on paying interest, on gambling with derivatives and options, and on investing in firms that make pornography or pork.[20]

Poverty Initiated Immigration

It is not surprising that the Muslim immigrant

invasion of Europe is primarily due to their poverty. They yearningly look to Europe, the richest, freest and securest continent on planet Earth. Poor people from Muslim countries desire some of these riches; that's the motivating reason for them to come, legally or illegally, to the European continent. But in order to fully participate in the success and prosperity of Europe, Muslims will have to adapt to European standards and culture, and not vice versa.

Global Migration

In times past, it was the Europeans who literally encircled the globe, establishing colonies and building nations. Now, the migration spirit is evident from Africa and Asia. An article published by *The New York Times*, 26 June 2010, reveals statistics showing the percentage of foreign-born people in various countries of the world for 2010. Here are a few examples:[21]

Britain	10%
Germany	13%
United States	14%
Canada	21%
Switzerland	23%

The trend of moving about was prophesied by Daniel, "Many shall run to and fro, and knowledge shall be increased" (Daniel 12:4). These facts undergird the building of a global community. Although there are flare-ups here and there, particularly against immigration, the tendency of integration nevertheless cannot be reversed. A global world society is clearly predicted in Holy Scripture; thus, we may expect even more immigration in the future.

Germany Needs Muslim Migrants

As already indicated, there are a great number of articles, reports, and books about the Muslim danger. But facts on the ground look quite different.

I have an article from a Düsseldorf newspaper, the *Rheinische Post*. The headline of a specific report reads: "SPD Leadership Protests Against ProNRW."

Here is the translation:

> SPD Party Chief Sigmar Gabriel challenged Muslims to stay in Germany, saying, 'We need you. Without the staying power of the immigrants, our society will be less capable in the future.'
>
> Gabriel opposed the anti-Islam declaration of renewal right party, ProNRW. He visited mosques in Oberhausen, Gelsenkirchen, Mülheim, Essen and Bochum. Party Chief

Sigmar Gabriel encouraged Muslims not to be intimidated by the threats of the new ProNRW Party.

Another leading SPD candidate, Hannelore Kraft, declared that she is proud of the excellent model behavior demonstrated between Germans and their Muslim neighbors in the city of Mülheim.

Furthermore, Party Chief Sigmar Gabriel, in communication with Muslims, promised a possible change of the present citizen rights. Immigrants (legal or illegal) who have lived in Germany 10 years or more should have the right to vote, regardless of their citizenship. Independent of citizenship, all people should have the right to vote where they live. Moreover, Gabriel insisted that schools, whether private or religious, should accept Muslim children. He stated all schools are supported or receive assistance from public funds and therefore are obligated to accommodate pupils from other religions.[22]

The threats made by various terrorist organizations are nothing other than soap bubbles, empty words, expressions of unbridled hate by religious fanatics who in reality have little power.

Soap Bubbles and Empty Words

When we analyze the innumerable media reports about the threats made by various terrorist organizations, we find that they are nothing other than soap bubbles, empty words, expressions of unbridled hate by religious fanatics who in reality have little power. If al Qaeda or any other terrorist organization really had the power to do irreparable damage to the USA or Europe, they most certainly would have done so long ago.

Satan's smart maneuvers focus the world's attention on Muslim terrorists, instead of the deceptive works within Churchianity, under the leadership of the spirit of Antichrist.

Terrorism Contributes to World Unity

Thus the question, why the use of so much time and so many resources to fight this powerless enemy? There is one answer: terrorism, real or imagined, is the driving force to unite the world. Never must we underestimate the clever deceptions of the father of lies, the great deceiver. Satan's smart maneuvers focus the world's attention on Muslim terrorists, instead of the deceptive works within Churchianity, under the leadership of the spirit of Antichrist.

Churchianity Dominates

What do we mean by Churchianity? Simply put, Christianity without Christ, those who are following the religion without a personal relationship with Jesus Christ the Lord.

Churchianity is revealed by our Lord in Matthew 7:20-23, "Wherefore by their fruits ye shall know them. Not every one that saith unto me, Lord, Lord, shall enter into the kingdom of heaven; but he that doeth the will of my Father which is in heaven. Many will say to me in that day, Lord, Lord, have we not prophesied in thy name? and in thy name have cast out devils? and in thy name done many wonderful works? And then will I profess unto them, I never knew you: depart from me, ye that work iniquity."

Satan, the father of lies, the murderer from the beginning, has been very successful in deceiving the nations of the world into believing that if they can defeat their imagined enemy, in this case, international terrorism, then the world can live in peace and security.

The last Gentile superpower is now in the process of being established in every country of the world.

CHAPTER 8

ANTICHRIST ON THE HORIZON

Religion is a major force supporting the rise of Antichrist, according to Scripture. Global economy and finance are already functioning. But unity must be established at any cost, and this includes religion.

The Real Truth

The Bible speaks of the coming peace in 1 Thessalonians 5:3: "For when they shall say, Peace and safety; then sudden destruction cometh upon them, as travail upon a woman with child; and they shall not escape." Who are "they"? The entire world. There will be peace, but it will be temporary and not real.

It is not going to be Muhammad, but Antichrist who will "confirm the covenant with many for one week: and in the midst of the week he shall cause the sacrifice and the oblation to cease...." That is why we are admonished throughout Scripture not to be entangled with this world, but to follow Him who says, "I am the truth."

John warns us: "Love not the world, neither the things that are in the world. If any man love the world, the love of the Father is not in him" (1 John 2:15).

Unity at Any Cost

Antichrist is anti-true Church, but not diametrically opposed on the surface.

John warns: "Little children, it is the last time: and as ye have heard that antichrist shall come, even now are there many antichrists; whereby we know that it is the last time" (1 John 2:18). This message is around 2,000 years old. It reinforces the fact that the spirit of Antichrist was at work during those days, and continues to be at work, even more so in these last days.

Will there be a one-world religion? Our answer is no. All religions will continue to operate within their own infrastructure.

What is his aim? To unite the world politically, economically, and religiously. That process has become more visible than ever before. When all is said and done, Revelation 13:8 will be fulfilled: "And all that dwell upon the earth shall worship him." The world will worship the image of the beast, the beast, and the dragon. That's just another reason why democracy is invading the Arab world. The Muslim's attention must be redirected to accommodate Churchianity, and vice versa.

One World Religion?

Does that mean there will be a one-world religion?

Our answer is no. All religions will continue to operate within their own infrastructure. Catholics will not become Protestant, Muslims will not become Hindu, Buddhists will not become Christian, but they all will agree that Antichrist is God, and subsequently worship him.

How religions can cooperate in the future is already foreshadowed by the world's economic and financial system.

One World Currency?

When it comes to finance, it's already global. Those who travel internationally care not what money they are dealing with, whether it's the euro, the British pound, the American dollar, the Japanese yen, or dozens of other national currencies. From that perspective, we already have a one world currency.

When using credit cards, one may travel all over the world and, in virtually any place, even in the most remote parts, major credit cards are accepted.

How is that possible? Isn't it a high risk for a credit company or a bank holding the account to allow people to travel all over the world and buy merchandise? What about the merchant, if he or she is crooked? Be assured, the credit card company has it figured out. They know how much money I have and how much I can spend. They know my financial history and they can rest in peace, knowing that I will pay the bill when it comes due.

The merchandiser, on the other hand, needs to be extremely careful. If he dare breach his contract only slightly with the credit card company, he will be heavily fined. Because of the relatively large percentage of income generated by purchases with credit cards, no merchant can afford to be dishonest. Granted, there are exceptions, but in general, that's not the case.

These things simply reinforce that global unity already exists today and will be more solidified in the days to come.

Is Integration Possible?

In the meantime, when it comes to the issue of Muslim dominance in Europe, we can assuredly say it will not happen. Europe is quite capable of accommodating diversity.

That is actually their motto, "United in Diversity."

From reports and testimonies, we learn that the process of integrating Muslims into the various European nations is well on its way.

Of course, there will always be a degree of separation, as for example in the United States: only Europeans are considered unqualified Americans. If you are of African descent, you are classified as African-American. Such is also the case if your ancestors came from Asia; you are Asian-American. Therefore, we may not expect full and equal integration of the nations, but rather a level of integration to accommodate "United in Diversity."

For God So Loved the World

One of the most important things for Christians to realize is, "For God so loved the world" (John 3:16). It does not identify a certain group of people, but the entire world. Consider therefore, the probability that it is God who caused the Muslims to come to Europe and the Latinos to North America. There is a specific purpose for that: they must hear the liberating Gospel of Jesus Christ our Lord!

Allow also for the possibility that because you

> *Allow for the possibility that because you were too comfortable to take the Gospel to foreign lands, the inhabitants of those lands are now coming to you!*

were too comfortable to take the Gospel to foreign lands, the inhabitants of those lands are now coming to you! Don't attempt to hide behind Satan's deception and say the Muslims are terrorists and the Latinos are ruining our country; that is following in the footsteps of the great deceiver. Rather, agree with the Word of God: "For God so loved the world, that he gave his only begotten Son, that whosoever believeth in him should not perish, but have everlasting life."

If God loves the world, which means all of humanity, then so should we. The one you reach with the Gospel may be the last from among the Gentiles. Romans 11:25-26 proclaims, "For I would not, brethren, that ye should be ignorant of this mystery, lest ye should be wise in your own conceits; that blindness in part is happened to Israel, until the fulness of the Gentiles be come in. And so all Israel shall be saved: as it is written, There shall come out of

Sion the Deliverer, and shall turn away ungodliness from Jacob."

This answers the question, when will salvation come to Israel? When "the fullness of the Gentiles [has] come in."

Many Muslims Turning to Jesus

We are happy to report that many Muslims are turning to the Lord and are becoming believers in Jesus. We deliberately do not mention names or places, which could endanger these new believers, but we can assuredly and with full confidence say that Jesus Christ is building His Church. He is using many of His faithful servants as tools in His hand to be messengers of the Good News to those who are rejected, downtrodden and despised. Therefore, let us herald loud and clear that Jesus saves and He is coming again soon!

CHAPTER 9

WHY THE WORLD MUST CHANGE

Since the beginning of the 1900s, the world has indeed changed, whether for good or evil. But change will continue for good and for evil, as discussed in this chapter. The world changes: only Jesus does not. He is the same yesterday, today and forever.

We are sinners by birth, and we must become saints by rebirth.

The Arab Change

"Democracy Invades Islam" simply means change. That change is now in progress. For one, it is changing the Arab world from dictatorship to democracy.

We have already dealt with a number of issues in the process of changing the Arab world, and that change will affect the rest of the world. But there is more that needs to be said.

Sinners Must Change to Saints

First of all, we must establish that change is ordered from God. For each individual on planet Earth, the most important change is changing our disposition. We are sinners by birth, and we must become saints by rebirth. We are flesh and blood, but we must become spiritual people. We are well entrenched in our family and nation, but we must become pilgrims and foreigners. Our life on earth should not serve self, but serve as preparation for eternity.

The Great Name Change

Jacob, the grandson of Abraham, left his homeland for a foreign country. On his way back to the Promised Land, he experienced a profound change.

We read in Genesis 32:27-28: "And he [an angel] said unto him, What is thy name? And he said, Jacob. And he said, Thy name shall be called no more Jacob, but Israel: for as a prince hast thou power with God and with men, and hast prevailed." Jacob, whose name literally means "supplanter" or "deceiver," receives a new name from the Lord—Israel, "fighter with God." That was the beginning of the name the nation carries today.

The Change of Garments

> *Our life on earth should not serve self, but serve as preparation for eternity.*

A few chapters further, we read of another change: "And God said unto Jacob, Arise, go up to Bethel, and dwell there: and make there an altar unto God, that appeared unto thee when thou fleddest from the face of Esau thy brother. Then Jacob said unto his household, and to all that were with him, Put away the strange gods that are among you, and be clean, and change your garments" (Genesis 35:1-

2). This change was required because Jacob and his family had to meet God through the altar of sacrifice.

This was a solemn request to change for the purpose of obtaining God's grace and protection. We read in verse 4: "And they gave unto Jacob all the strange gods which were in their hand, and all their earrings which were in their ears; and Jacob hid them under the oak which was by Shechem."

What was the result of this change? We have the answer in verse 5: "And they journeyed: and the terror of God was upon the cities that were round about them, and they did not pursue after the sons of Jacob."

There are many other changes we read of the Old Testament, but all these changes were primarily outward and pointed to the change that would take place within the heart of man.

The Changing of the Covenant

The prophet Jeremiah spoke of a New Covenant in about 600 BC: "Behold, the days come, saith the LORD, that I will make a new covenant with the house of Israel, and with the house of Judah" (Jeremiah 31:31).

The most important ingredient of the New Covenant was the change of the inner person. Jeremiah explains: "But this shall be the covenant that I will make with the house of Israel; After those days, saith the LORD, I will put my law in their inward parts, and write it in their hearts; and will be their God, and they shall be my people. And they shall teach no more every man his neighbour, and every man his brother, saying, Know the LORD: for they shall all know me, from the least of them unto the greatest of them, saith the LORD: for I will forgive their iniquity, and I will remember their sin no more" (verses 33-34).

That's the great change; it would not require Israel to keep the many laws in order to please God, but the New Covenant would please God so that Israel could do the will of God.

Change Based on the Blood

The Old Covenant is built upon the shedding of the blood of animals, which the Bible tells us could never take away sins. It only covered the sins of the people temporarily. The New Covenant is based on the shed blood of the Son of God: "So Christ was once offered to bear the sins of many;

and unto them that look for him shall he appear the second time without sin unto salvation" (Hebrews 9:28).

When in the fullness of time Jesus came, He fulfilled in every detail all requirements to seal the New Covenant. That's when the great change had begun, the change from temporary to eternal, the change of earthly to heavenly.

The Blotting Out of Sin

The Apostle Peter speaks of that fulfillment to the Jews in Jerusalem when he says, "But those things, which God before had shewed by the mouth of all his prophets, that Christ should suffer, he hath so fulfilled. Repent ye therefore, and be converted, that your sins may be blotted out, when the times of refreshing shall come from the presence of the Lord" (Acts 3:18-19). Note the difference from the covering of sins to the "blotting out" of sins. This change had not been fulfilled as a one-time event, but has continued now for almost 2,000 years.

Israel's Coming Change

Although the foundation of the Church and the first members were all Jews, the collective promise of the whole nation being converted had not taken place at that time.

Here is what we read in Acts 15:13-15: "And after they had held their peace, James answered, saying, Men and brethren, hearken unto me: Simeon hath declared how God at the first did visit the Gentiles, to take out of them a people for his name. And to this agree the words of the prophets." This is fulfillment of prophecy. Before the regeneration of all Israel takes place, the fullness of the Gentiles has to come in. That is why verse 14 says, "God at the first did visit the Gentiles."

Before the regeneration of all Israel takes place, the fullness of the Gentiles has to come in.

Fullness of the Gentiles

This seems like a contradiction, because we just stated that the foundation and the members of the first church were all Jews. However, reading carefully, we note that this is referring to Israel's collective salvation, not individual salvation. The Apostle Paul writes in Romans 11:25-26:

"...blindness in part is happened to Israel, until the fulness of the Gentiles be come in. And so all Israel shall be saved: as it is written, There shall come out of Sion the Deliverer, and shall turn away ungodliness from Jacob."

What will happen after the fullness of the Gentiles has come in, after God has taken out a people from the Gentiles for His name? Acts 15:16 will be fulfilled: "After this I will return, and will build again the tabernacle of David, which is fallen down; and I will build again the ruins thereof, and I will set it up." This speaks of the physical and literal reestablishment of the Jewish State in the land of Israel.

When Jesus returns to the Mount of Olives in Israel, a number of changes will take place.

Topographical Change

When Jesus returns to the Mount of Olives in Israel, a number of changes will take place. For one thing, there will be a topographical change, "And his feet shall stand in that day upon the mount of Olives, which is before Jerusalem on the east, and the mount of Olives shall cleave in the midst thereof toward the east and toward the west, and there shall be a very great valley; and half of the mountain shall remove toward the north, and half of it toward the south" (Zechariah 14:4). We all agree this has not yet taken place.

Something extraordinary must happen for these carnivores to become vegetarians. This demolishes the Preterist theology, which insists that all prophecies were fulfilled in the first century.

Change of All Creatures

Isaiah reports: "The wolf and the lamb shall feed together, and the lion shall eat straw like the bullock: and dust shall be the serpent's meat. They shall not hurt nor destroy in all my holy mountain, saith the LORD" (Isaiah 65:25). There has to be a drastic change for the wolf and the lamb to feed together, and the lion to eat straw. Something extraordinary must happen for these carnivores to become vegetarians. This demolishes the Preterist theology, which insists that all prophecies were fulfilled in the first century.

We note that the serpent will finally eat dust.

That was the original curse upon the serpent, "...dust shalt thou eat all the days of thy life" (Genesis 3:14). But lo and behold, the serpent did not eat dust. We all know that the serpent (snake) eats frogs, mice, rats, rabbits, and even some larger animals. But when the great change comes, the serpent will finally eat dust. The serpent will no longer be a carnivore, nor will it become a vegetarian, but an "earthatarian." That's something totally new—living on dust.

The Apostle Paul speaks of this coming great change: "For the earnest expectation of the creature waiteth for the manifestation of the sons of God. For the creature was made subject to vanity, not willingly, but by reason of him who hath subjected the same in hope, because the creature itself also shall be delivered from the bondage of corruption into the glorious liberty of the children of God. For we know that the whole creation groaneth and travaileth in pain together until now" (Romans 8:19-22).

Change of Environment

There are innumerable organizations and movements the world over dedicated to the preservation of the world's resources, its vegetation, waters, and animal life. We call them environmentalists. What is their object? In brief, to make this world a better place to live for all. That, we must agree, is a noble thing. In spite of much criticism, the environmentalists have achieved some quite remarkable results. Those of us who lived through the 50s and 60s can recall how our rivers were polluted, the skies were darkened with clouds of ash, and other pollution was being spewed out by factories. We witnessed the dying of forests.

There are innumerable organizations and movements the world over dedicated to the preservation of the world's resources, its vegetation, waters, and animal life.

One instance I must relate was in 1968 in Hamilton, Ohio. Not far from where we lived, the Armco Steel plant was operating. My wife Ruth, who always believed in (and still does) drying her wash outside on a line, experienced occasionally when the wind blew in the "wrong direction," that the newly washed clothes were polluted with ash particles and had to be

The world will yet experience the final great pollution, which is recorded for us in the book of Revelation.

rewashed. A small river close by, the *Little Miami*, always carried a bad odor and, rather frequently, fish were seen floating belly up, killed by pollution.

Today, these things have changed—not only in the United States, but in most industrial countries of the world. Thus, we must give credit where credit is due: the environmentalists have definitely contributed toward a cleaner environment. That, of course, does not mean we endorse their agenda, but neither do we oppose it.

The Greatest Pollution Yet to Come

We must emphasize that the success of some of the environmentalists' projects is temporary, because the world will yet experience the final great pollution, which is recorded for us in the book of Revelation. Let us just quote some of the events that will take place when the trumpet judgments are executed upon planet Earth:

"The first angel sounded, and there followed hail and fire mingled with blood, and they were cast upon the earth: and the third part of trees was burnt up, and all green grass was burnt up. And the second angel sounded, and as it were a great mountain burning with fire was cast into the sea: and the third part of the sea became blood; and the third part of the creatures which were in the sea, and had life, died; and the third part of the ships were destroyed. And the third angel sounded, and there fell a great star from heaven, burning as it were a lamp, and it fell upon the third part of the rivers, and upon the fountains of waters; And the name of the star is called Wormwood: and the third part of the waters became wormwood; and many men died of the waters, because they were made bitter" (Revelation 8:7-11). That's not man-made, but God-made.

Change of the Gentile World

His coming also spells the end of all Gentile power. From that point on, Jesus will rule with a rod of iron. That means the period of grace has ended for the nations. Now, for the first time in history, the nations will be subject to the law of righteousness. Then will be implemented what is written, "The soul that sinneth, it shall die."

There will no longer be enemies of Israel, no anti-Semites secretly or publicly.

Zechariah reveals the change that will come upon the Gentiles: "Thus saith the LORD of hosts; In those days it shall come to pass, that ten men shall take hold out of all languages of the nations, even shall take hold of the skirt of him that is a Jew, saying, We will go with you: for we have heard that God is with you" (Zechariah 8:23).

From that point on, there will no longer be enemies of Israel, no anti-Semites secretly or publicly because the nations will then have understood what Jesus said, "Salvation is of the Jews." They will seek favor because, "we have heard that God is with you."

Gun Laws Will Change

When Jesus rules, He will implement peace because He is the Prince of Peace. This will not be attained by a new system, but was paid for by Jesus Christ Himself, "And, having made peace through the blood of his cross, by him to reconcile all things unto himself; by him, I say, whether they be things in earth, or things in heaven" (Colossians 1:20). Let no one ever say that our military brought us peace and freedom. That is an insult to the entire work of redemption Jesus accomplished on Calvary's Cross. When He comes to planet Earth, He will abolish the military with all its weapons, as is documented by the prophet Micah: "And he shall judge among many people, and rebuke strong nations afar off; and they shall beat their swords into plowshares, and their spears into pruninghooks: nation shall not lift up a sword against nation, neither shall they learn war any more" (Micah 4:3).

When He comes to planet Earth, He will abolish the military with all its weapons.

Global Political Change

Contributing to this change is democracy, which is now taking the world by storm. That, however, does not mean that all nations will become equal. There are many types of democracy today, and so it will be in the future.

Some ask, what about China? Experts predict China will become the largest economy in the

> *All will agree that this new global political system, yet to be identified, is humanity's only hope.*

world. That nation is ruled by communism. But the type of communism China practices is clearly patterned after the will of the people; thus, we may call it another form of democracy. We must not assume that all nations of the world will follow the guidelines of European or American-style democracy.

Here again, the motto, "United in Diversity" will be applied. While the extreme capitalist democracy of the United States is being changed into a social capital democracy, China's communist philosophy is being changed into a social communist democracy. What we must keep in mind when analyzing these things is not to expect a drastic and instant change of the entire world into some form of one world government. However, all will agree that this new global political system, yet to be identified, is humanity's only hope (albeit a false one).

Hundred Years of Change

When we compare the world just 100 years ago

with today, we can speak of mind-boggling change. The nations of the world, at the beginning of the 1900s, adamantly opposed any kind of internationalism. European colonial powers were fiercely protecting their conquered territory. They used their military strength to insure that the colonies remain loyal to their "mother country."

But then, the colonial times ended. The colonies wanted change, so they rebelled; they insisted on change, on independence. That was part of the ongoing global change. Today, we are experiencing some fascinating and disturbing changes, as we record in the next chapter.

CHAPTER 10

THE GREAT CHANGE OF PROGRESSIVE GLOBALISM

This chapter may be the most controversial one due to the simple fact that change must continue globally, and that particularly the USA lags dangerously behind when it comes to change.

Changing the USA

In the United States, the word globalism is looked upon with mistrust, particularly by the "right" leaning spectrum of the population, of whom many assume that globalism will rob America of its independence and encroach upon its freedom. That, indeed, is true. But to be a member of the global family, international laws and regulations must be adhered to. Yet, that type of change requires a degree of sacrifice of sovereignty, and many Americans are still uncomfortable with this development. Experts agree that without full cooperation in the global economy, the United States could not exist as an independent nation operating in a civilized manner. That's the simple truth.

Changing Europe

One of the most remarkable occurrences in the process of change has taken place on the European continent. At the time of writing, 27 nations are members of the European Union. They have created the world's largest economy. They are the biggest exporters and importers.

But there is more to come. Dozens of nations are

standing in line, application in hand, hoping to become members of the European Union.

The criteria to become a member of the Union is somewhat complicated, but suffice it to say, these are fundamental human rights, democracy and adherence to a number of international treaties. The applying nation must produce evidence that they can operate a functioning economy and control their own financial system. Most importantly, they must be capable of change.

That is often difficult, because these various European nations have ancient histories that predate the colonies that were established on the American continent. They were functioning nations, using their own language and practicing their own culture and tradition. Yet, they must continue to change; in EU-speak, they must meet "convergence criteria" until it becomes evident what Revelation 17:13 says: "These have one mind, and shall give their power and strength unto the beast."

The Change That Made America Great

Change was something that America historically practiced extremely well. The diverse group of primarily European immigrants changed into a solid, united and prosperous nation. While the European nations were continually fighting each other, the newly established United States of America offered an alternative—unity. Although during the heyday of mass immigration arriving on the shores of America, certain enclaves evolved—Italians, Russians, Irish, Germans, and others tried to stick together—it did not last long until all were dissolved into one identity—Americans.

This was a contributing cause for many educated and rich Europeans to come to the new country, where the threat of war was not hanging over their heads.

Slowdown of Change

However, America's progress of change slowed down to a virtual halt after the Second World War. A contributing factor was the general perception that anything not 100 percent American was considered anti-American. That was the seed sown particularly by anti-communist, anti-socialist and anti-foreigner rhetoric, now growing to fruition. Today, it seems all but impossible to implement fundamental changes in American society. In the meantime, many prosperous socialist nations are beginning to leave the USA behind.

The Great Brain Drain

It was in 1964 when I was residing in Perth, Western Australia, that I read the headline in the local paper about the great brain drain from Britain. This story claimed that over 20,000 British engineers were migrating to the United States annually. The writer of the article expressed his concern about Britain's future in being able to compete in the industrialized world. America represented hope and the future.

Today, this has changed. America has become a semi-cheap labor country; subsequently, thousands of European and Asian firms have moved their factories to the United States, primarily due to "cheap labor cost." That is a long-term real problem, because cheap labor will produce cheap products.

Global Outsourcing

Under hourly compensation, ventureoutsource.com published figures from the Bureau of Labor Statistics with the introduction:[23]

Manufacturing hourly compensation costs were highest in Norway, at 1.8 times the U.S. level. Australia, Canada and 10 of the 12 European countries had higher hourly compensation costs than the United States. Spain and Portugal were the only two European countries that had lower hourly compensation than the United States.

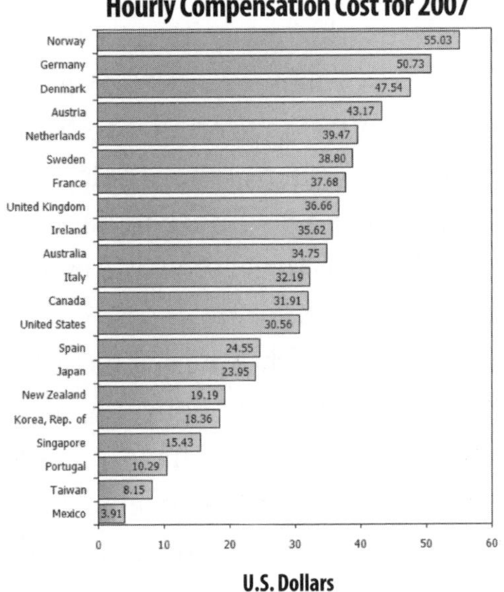

Quite striking is the fact that of the ten highest labor cost countries, nine are European. Realizing that these nations are mainly from the territory of the ancient Roman World Empire, we may justifiable speak of the resurrection of Rome as the final Gentile superpower.

International Treaties

One can find a number of international treaties and agreements which the US is not a signatory to. Here are just a few examples:

- The Convention on the Elimination of All Forms of Discrimination Against Women (CEDAW)
- The Convention on the Rights of the Child (CRC)
- The Convention on the Prohibition, Use, Stockpiling, Production and Transfer of Anti-Personnel Mines and on Their Destruction (The Ottawa Treaty)
- Kyoto Protocol
- The International Criminal Court (ICC)
- International Labor Organization (ILO) Conventions
- The International Covenant on Economic, Social and Cultural Rights (ICESCR)
- International Convention on the Protection of the Rights of All Migrant Workers and Members of Their Families (MWC)

It is important to mention here that this author

neither endorses nor objects to any and all treaties. Our focus remains a biblical worldview and we do not intend to support or hinder any of these and other international treaties on the books now. The reason for publishing this information is simply to show that the United States will continue to experience extreme difficulty in implementing fundamental changes, which in turn will contribute to the accelerated decline of America's global influence.

Antiquated Measurements

The most obvious sign of America's unwillingness to change is its antiquated measurement system. While the whole world, without exception, changed to the metric system, the United States still makes use of the ancient, outmoded European system of miles, yards, inches, gallons, quarts, pints, pounds, ounces, etc.

The country once leading the world in change and founded upon the insistence on change, is now left behind, stuck in the old European systems.

Granted, this may not be of great significance, but it does show the tendency of the United States to balk at change.

Change in Energy Consumption

An extremely important issue for the United States is change in energy consumption. Countries with an equivalent or higher standard of living use significantly less energy than Americans per capita.

European and Asian countries were quick to change, realizing that energy will continue to be scarce with each passing year.

Although significant progress has been made in reducing energy consumption in the United States, America still lags far behind other progressive nations. While the country represents only five percent of the world's population, it consumes almost 25 percent of the world's energy. That is one of the greatest problems America faces.

Country or Region	Energy used in 2008	Population in 2008
World total	**492.6 quadrillion BTU (100%)**	**6,700 million (100%)**
United States	120.9 quadrillion BTU (24.5%)	305 million (4.5%)
China	85.1 quadrillion BTU (17.2%)	1,325 million (19%)
Europe	85.9 quadrillion BTU (17.4%)	736 million (11%)

Sources: US Energy Administration,[24] Population Reference Bureau[25]

Energy and the Arabs

You may think that speaking of energy and excessive consumption may not be directly relate to "democracy invading Islam," but not when we realize that the Islamic nations are the major holders of energy resources. There is definitely a link between the production and consumption of energy. Will America change in its thirst for energy? Most likely not, at least not in the foreseeable future.

Cheap Gasoline the Real Problem?

This paragraph I'm writing may cause some to stop reading this book. Why? Because America's main problem is not the much-sensationalized news about the rising cost of gasoline at the pump, but the comparatively cheap energy we are being supplied with. Although it's impossible to say how the following figures will look a few months down the road, they do reflect gasoline prices in 2010.

Comparing 1965 with 2010

In 1965, the minimum wage was $1.25 per hour. The cost of one gallon of gas was about 32 cents. That means, 15 minutes of work for one gallon of gasoline. In 2010, the minimum wage stood at $7.25 per hour, and gasoline stood at $3.23/gallon. That means, a half hour of work for one gallon of gasoline. But that's not where the comparison ends. The motor vehicle in 1965 averaged about 11 miles per gallon, while today's average is 25 miles per gallon. That simply means transportation from point A to B is cheaper today than it was in 1965.

Other comparisons are even more dramatic, such as tires, batteries, and the vehicle itself. One cannot find a reasonable correlation when it comes to the cars of today. Those sold in 1965 were definitely inferior to the modern day automobile. The 1965 model car was a heavy piece of steel, powered with an insufficient 8-cylinder motor. It had no air conditioning, and only the upgraded models would have an AM-FM radio with one speaker. Not to mention the dangerous engineering—no collapsible steering, no air bags, and the seatbelts that were installed in some models were actually never used. If you were to add the cost of the standard features in today's modern automobile, you simply would have to give up because there is no comparison. Yet, the average cost of the car was about the same—one year's wages, not to mention the fact that the 1965 car would not be expected to operate beyond 100,000 miles. Today, a car with that same amount of miles could be considered virtually "new."

Without effective public transportation, America has grown totally dependent on private motor vehicles and, despite improving gas mileage, most prefer larger ones—pickup trucks, SUVs and minivans. Why? Would you believe it's because of cheap gasoline?

Furthermore, houses are much larger today than those built in 1965. This means more space, more energy consumption. In summary, one of America's greatest problems is cheap energy. But most of us would vigorously deny such simple facts.

Taxing Gasoline

In comparison, most progressive nations pay double, even triple the amount for energy that Americans do. Gasoline is heavily taxed in Europe. For example, in Germany in 2009, tax stood at €0.654 per liter (approximately $3.60 per gallon).[26] When you factor in the Value Added Tax (19%) on the fuel itself and the Fuel Tax, the tax alone added up to €1.22 per liter ($6.28 per gallon). Even in Norway, the third largest oil exporter, $1.42 tax per liter ($5.36 per gallon) was added.[27] Although the tax rate varies greatly from country to country, most nations pay a high price for their gasoline. Furthermore, those who own vehicles with large engines must pay additional tax in some countries.

The progressive nations quickly learned that, if the cost were high, the people would be careful when consuming energy. Most of the richest nations in the world pay $7 to $10 per gallon.

Besides driving innovation in fuel economy, these taxes also provide a buffer for the government; they could be temporarily suspended. The US only has a 40-50 cent buffer to work with.

Add $3-4 Tax Per Gallon?

The problem is worse than most think. America insists on not changing. No politician in their right mind would suggest $3-4 additional tax on a gallon of gasoline. That politician would not stand a chance to be reelected. So, when it comes to playing the blame game, I think we would do well to look in the mirror to see the culprit of America's greatest problem.

Will America change? Very unlikely. But the astronomical thirst for imported oil is upsetting the balance sheet to dangerous levels. What will happen when communist China, Japan and socialist Europe no longer buy US government bonds to underwrite this lopsided consumption?

The astronomical thirst for imported oil is upsetting the balance sheet to dangerous levels.

Abundance of Oil?

The majority of the United States' citizens seem to be living in an illusion, believing that energy is unlimited, without consciously realizing that the largest portion of the energy has to be imported, mostly from Islamic nations.

For many decades, we have received reports our readers sent in where the authors tried to show that there is an abundance of oil in the United States; subsequently, no need for oil imports.

In the March 2011 issue of *Midnight Call*, we published a letter from one of our readers. The following is an excerpt:

> I encountered a book several years ago written by Jerome R. Corsi, Ph.D., called, *Black Gold Stranglehold—The Myth of*

> *Scarcity and the Politics of Oil*, which exposes the fraudulent science that has been sold to the world in order to enslave them: the belief that oil is a fossil fuel and a finite resource.
>
> The book goes into great detail on how the oil producing nations manipulate world economies, use rogue terrorist regimes like Libya for their own ends, and act as our friend while we buy their oil, and then work behind our back to destroy our way of life.
>
> Simply stated, there is growing evidence that we, in fact, are not running out of oil. If we are not, then there should not be any mad dash to drill for new oil to quench the global appetite. At this point in history, there are more proven oil reserves than ever, despite many decades of increased consumption. So, if we are using more because of the thousands of cars being built in China, India, Indonesia, etc., but in fact, oil is not being decreased in any capacity, then perhaps we are being hoodwinked into believing exactly what the environmental extremists want us to believe.

Worldometers reveals that 51 million new cars were put on the roads in 2009.

Sounds convincing doesn't it? Obviously, it is dead wrong. First of all, China, India, Indonesia, etc., are not adding "thousands of cars" every year to their roads, but tens of millions. Worldometers reveals that 51 million new cars were put on the roads in 2009. Simply put, more oil is required to satisfy the thirst of these vehicles.

Oil Below the Ocean Floor

The reason these giant oil companies drill in such awkward and dangerous places is proof that there is not enough to be found on land.

Moreover, many of the major newly discovered oil fields are located in the ocean. It is relatively easy to set up an oilrig on the land in a year, but extremely difficult, dangerous, and very expensive to do the same in the water. British Petroleum, known today as BP, almost went bankrupt when one of its towers blew up in the Gulf of Mexico—and there is more to come regarding financial assessment. The reason these giant oil companies drill in such awkward and dangerous places is proof that there is not enough to be found on land.

The Coming Arab Energy Power Play

How does this all relate to *Democracy Invades Islam*? As already stated, Islamic countries are the holders of the world's largest oil reservoirs. Presently, the West is dealing primarily with dictators who can be easily swayed with large amounts of cash. But when democracy takes hold of the Arab nations, the people will insist on participating in the oil wealth; subsequently, energy costs cannot go anywhere but up.

After the Arab nations have implemented democracy, the world will definitely look different.

Oil Lubricates Global Unity

America's predicament will doubtless assist the Arab aspiration to become more democratic and be able to have a more significant voice when it comes to the cost of oil. That is another step closer toward equality among the nations of the world. The long neglected and looked down upon Arab world is arising for a specific purpose: to be counted as an equal partner in the global economy.

CHAPTER 11

RELIGION AND POLITICS

While this chapter may not deal directly with our title, *Democracy Invades Islam,* it does highlight the important issue of government and religion. The largest oil reservoir is in the hands of Islam. The greatest financial and economic power is in the hands of traditionally Christian countries. We will discuss how the mixture between politics and religion plays a major role in the end times in this chapter.

Government and the Church

"Submit yourselves to every ordinance of man for the Lord's sake: whether it be to the king, as supreme; or unto governors, as unto them that are sent by him for the punishment of evildoers, and for the praise of them that do well...Honour all men. Love the brotherhood. Fear God. Honour the king" (1 Peter 2:13-14, 17).

The instruction for the Church is crystal clear: obey the government. Thus, we must outright reject the insistence that the Church is part of the government.

The Apostle Peter introduces the relationship between the Church and the government with the words, "Dearly beloved, I beseech you as strangers and pilgrims" (1 Peter 2:11). This demolishes the well-established theory of a "Christian nation." Holy Scripture invalidated such a notion; there never was and never will be a "Christian nation."

When we grasp these important fundamental truths, we will not be moved by every wind of doctrine that comes and goes.

The Apostle Paul too, inspired by the Holy Spirit, instructs the Church: "Let every soul be subject unto the higher powers. For there is no power but of God: the powers that be are ordained of God" (Romans 13:1). Scripture should settle all remaining questions regarding the Church's relationship to the government and vice versa.

> *Nationalists insist that the Church is somehow responsible and duty bound to assist, guide, and direct the affairs of the government.*

Christians Are Strangers and Aliens in This World

To understand the position of the Church in the world is extremely important. Although we will not deal with this matter in detail in this book, I suggest that every Christian carefully examine the statements made by nationalists who insist that the Church is somehow responsible and duty bound to assist, guide, and direct the affairs of the government. That spirit is foreign to the collective teaching of the New Testament.

Religion and Religious Laws

When government interferes with religion or religion with government, it results in extreme brutality. Jon Meacham in his book, *American*

Gospel, writes about colonial America on page 43:

> The 'Laws Divine, Moral and Martial' were severe, legislating religious observance 'upon pain of death.' Those who failed to come to services twice daily would first lose their food for the day. A second offense brought a whipping, and a third six months in the gallows. To break the Sabbath 'by any gaming, public or private' or to miss church on Sunday was, on the third offense, a capital crime.[28]

On page 53, he speaks of Connecticut and New England:

> To the north the news was worse. 'If any man shall have or worship any God but the Lord God, he shall be put to death,' it said. Reviewing the history of the New England colonies, Tocqueville remarked that 'the legislator, forgetting completely the great principles of religious liberty he himself demanded in Europe, forces attendance at divine service by fear of fines, and he goes as far as to strike with severe penalties, and often death, Christians who wish to worship God according to a form other than his.'[29]

These things are not a secret. We use the very words of the so-called pilgrims and, later on, the Founding Fathers. Today, some ministers loudly proclaim, "Take back America...Reclaim America for Christ...Turn America back to its beginning, etc." Do they really want to grant religion the authority to implement laws? Would anyone like to see their spouse, son or daughter put to death because they don't worship the Lord God? Interestingly, these same nationalists vehemently object to the Muslims implementing their religious laws.

Government Separation from Religion

Later, the Founding Fathers, of whom many were Deists and Freemasons, changed colonial laws by an amendment to the Constitution, "Congress shall make no law respecting an establishment of religion, or prohibiting the free exercise thereof."

Under the subject "Church and State," Wikipedia writes:

> The concept of separation of church and state refers to the distance in the relationship between organized religion and the nation state. The term is an offshoot of the phrase, 'wall of separation between church and state,' as written in Thomas Jefferson's letter to the Danbury Baptists Association in 1802. The original text reads: "... I contemplate with sovereign reverence that act of the whole American people which declared that their legislature should 'make no law respecting an establishment of religion, or prohibiting the free exercise thereof,' thus building a wall of separation between Church & State."[30]

Obviously, this was an answer to the Vatican doctrine, which united church and state, preferable with the church having the upper hand.

Evangelicals Support Roman Doctrine

Lately, in the United States, we hear many voices of well meaning and often Gospel believing preachers proclaiming the need to "return America to its roots." One well-known preacher wrote to "advocate for the return of righteousness to American life." In other words, insisting on Vatican doctrine: a Christian nation.

"Return of righteousness" indicates that at some point in history, America was righteous.

To read such a statement from a passionate evangelical leader reveals that there are those who have gone way past the authority and commission of the Church of Jesus Christ. "Return of righteousness" indicates that at some point in history, America was righteous, but such insistence is anti-Holy Bible. Scripture clearly reveals our righteousness, "But we are all as an unclean thing, and all our righteousnesses are as filthy rags; and we all do fade as a leaf; and our iniquities, like the wind, have taken us away" (Isaiah 64:6).

Political Righteousness?

Whatever type of "righteousness" the preacher means, a black person, a slave and women who had virtually no rights would most certainly not want to "return" to this type of "righteousness."

American history proves beyond a shadow of a doubt that America never was a Christian nation—and, we must add, it never will be.

This clearly shows that when we allow ourselves to be tempted into Lucifer's territory, we will become his servants instead of fulfilling the commission of our Lord Jesus Christ.

One does not need to be a scholar on American history to prove beyond a shadow of a doubt that America never was a Christian nation—and, we must add, it never will be.

Misusing Scripture

The mistake made by these political evangelicals is

The Church cannot be the state, neither can the state be the Church. These two identities are diametrically opposed to each other.

due to the religious nature of the people and leaders during the early days of the colonies, and later when the states were established. Biblical references such as Almighty, salvation, God, even the name Jesus Christ, in no way indicate that the person is a true servant of the Lord Jesus Christ, born again of His Spirit.

The excessive brutality of the so-called pilgrims and the religious dictatorial authority of some colonies, clearly and in unmistakable terms demonstrate fanatical religious activity without the true center of the Gospel of Jesus Christ, whose entire work can be summarized with one word: love. We must insist, the Church cannot be the state, neither can the state be the Church. These two identities are diametrically opposed to each other.

Love Your Enemies

We do well to heed the Word of God precisely in this matter; we obey the prevailing government, but we are not the government. The mixing of religion and politics is a clever maneuver of the great deceiver. The Church cannot become part of this world, neither can the world become part of the Church. The true Church must fulfill its calling to be salt and light on earth: in love, compassion and self-sacrifice, not to be the political power.

The mixing of religion and politics is a clever maneuver of the great deceiver. The Church cannot become part of this world, neither can the world become part of the Church.

The very fact that Jesus says, "Love your enemies, bless them that curse you, do good to them that hate you, and pray for them which despitefully use you, and persecute you" (Matthew 5:44), clearly demonstrates that no government in the world could function practicing Jesus' words. To implement the teachings of Jesus Christ our Lord would invalidate all perception of law and order for any political identity.

The Church is a very unique identity and is found all over the world, but that Church must

To implement the teachings of Jesus Christ our Lord would invalidate all perception of law and order for any political identity.

not be confused with institutional organizations, by whatever name. Only true believers, born again of the Spirit of God, constitute the true Church on earth, of which Jesus stated, "I will build my church."

How is the Church Jesus builds to present itself? Be sure to read the next chapter.

CHAPTER 12

SATAN'S CLEVER DEVICES

To realize the purpose and calling of the Church of Jesus Christ on earth will result in the unmasking of the real enemy, Satan, and the spiritual powers of darkness.

While we do not directly concern ourselves with democracy invading Islam in this chapter, we are emphasizing the essential distinction of the true Church of Jesus Christ.

As born again believers, we may be insignificant, plain people like anyone else. There is no halo around our head or some unique outward appearance signifying our special position.

War Against the Flesh

Let us see from biblical perspectives how Christians are involved in this invisible struggle against the powers of darkness: "For we wrestle not against flesh and blood, but against principalities, against powers, against the rulers of the darkness of this world, against spiritual wickedness in high places" (Ephesians 6:12). This is not against any political ruler, whoever he may be. We are involved in a spiritual battle, "against the rulers of the darkness of this world."

Who are these rulers of darkness? They are the enemies of our spirit; they wish to silence our testimony. They try desperately to extinguish the **light** and cause the **salt** to be ineffective. Christians are the light of the world, they are the salt of the earth, Jesus stated. When we accept truth and practice truth in our own personal life, we are **light** and we are **salt.**

> *The devil's aim is to incite the old nature to rule the new nature.*

As born again believers, we may be insignificant, plain people like anyone else. There is no halo around our head or some unique outward appearance signifying our special position. However, what is within us is the essential part. John writes: "Whosoever is born of God doth not commit sin; for his seed remaineth in him: and he cannot sin, because he is born of God" (1 John 3:9). The new person born within me is perfect, "he cannot sin."

Unfortunately, this new person is housed in the old nature, the old tabernacle, and is subject to sin. Paul states, "...we have this treasure in earthen vessels..." (2 Corinthians 4:7). That is why 1 John 3:8 reads: "He that committeth sin is of the devil; for the devil sinneth from the beginning." That's the real battle we are involved in; our outward person is subject to sin, but our inner person, the newborn creature in Christ, is perfect and sinless.

The devil's aim is to incite the old nature to rule the new nature. The Apostle Paul confirms this in Galatians 5:17: "For the flesh lusteth against the

Spirit, and the Spirit against the flesh: and these are contrary the one to the other: so that ye cannot do the things that ye would." When the devil is successful at this, he has obliterated the true testimony; the true light and the true salt become clouded or ineffective.

How to Stand

What must we do? Read carefully Ephesians chapter 6, and notice the word "stand." For example, in verse 11: "Put on the whole armour of God, that ye may be able to **stand** against the wiles of the devil." We are not to attack; if we do, we are going to lose, but when we stand on the truth of the Word of God, we become untouchable from the evil one.

Verses 13-14 confirm the need for standing: "Wherefore take unto you the whole armour of God, that ye may be able to **withstand** in the evil day, and having done all, to **stand. Stand** therefore, having your loins girt about with truth, and having on the breastplate of righteousness."

Many servants of the Lord with good intentions have fallen prey to the devil's devices, namely the direct confrontation against the rulers of darkness of this world. As a result, they have lost their authority and testimony as servants of our Lord Jesus Christ. They are no longer effective **light** and **salt.**

Everlasting Life, Now and Later

Let us further emphasize our spiritual position. Every child who has gone to Sunday School can recite John 3:16: "For God so loved the world, that he gave his only begotten Son, that whosoever believeth in him should not perish, but have everlasting life." Note the last sentence, "have everlasting life." Yet, believers die. Each of us who believe will die eventually, unless the Rapture takes place first. Hebrews 9:27 is applicable to all people: "And as it is appointed unto men once to die, but after this the judgment." Therefore, when the Bible says, "have everlasting life," it means the new creature in Christ, not our flesh and blood nature.

> *We must learn to distinguish between our earthly, physical life and our spiritual life.*

Thus, we must learn to distinguish between our

earthly, physical life and our spiritual life.

Our spiritual person is already connected through the Holy Spirit to heaven: "And hath raised us up together, and made us sit together in heavenly places in Christ Jesus" (Ephesians 2:6). Philippians 3:20 continues: "For our conversation is in heaven; from whence also we look for the Saviour, the Lord Jesus Christ." This is a spiritual reality. Believing and practicing this truth causes our light to shine before others, and we become effective light and salt to our surroundings.

Spiritual Comes First

Furthermore, our Lord Jesus Christ reveals the reality of the spiritual life in His High-Priestly Prayer, "I have glorified thee on the earth: I have finished the work which thou gavest me to do" (John 17:4). From physical perspectives, He had not finished the work; He had not even been arrested, condemned, or crucified on Calvary's Cross; He had not died, neither had He risen or ascended to the Father, yet He prays, "I have finished the work which thou gavest me to do." This confirms that obedience is fulfillment. Abraham was obedient and the Bible says, "By faith

Abraham...offered up Isaac." Did he in real life? No, but obedience is counted as fulfillment.

Making Sinners Out of Saints

This should help us in analyzing the things that are happening on earth in light of the spiritual things in heavenly places, that is, in the invisible world. The same thing is happening for the rest of the world. This also includes the activity from below: the demons of the powers of darkness are busy transforming sinners into worshipers of Satan. That is the devil's goal. His aim is to seal every person on planet Earth with the mark of the beast, thereby declaring to God, "This one is mine, eternally doomed!"

The demons of the powers of darkness are busy transforming sinners into worshipers of Satan.

Satan Answers Prayer

Every government of every nation in the world, whether it's democracy, communism, dictatorship, or monarchy, they all want the best for their people; they loudly proclaim, "We want peace, prosperity, and security for our citizens!" Satan will gladly answer that prayer, and that's what all of world history is about—preparation for eternal doom on the one hand, and preparation for eternal salvation on the other.

In order for the devil to be successful, he must bring the nations of the world closer together. That's why the Arab world must be brought into the camp of the people-power democracy. Keep Satan's goal in mind, for the Bible warns us, "Lest Satan should get an advantage of us: for we are not ignorant of his devices" (2 Corinthians 2:11).

CHAPTER 13

ORIGIN AND AIM OF THE DECEIVER

We continue to highlight the position of the true Church of Jesus Christ on earth and what we are to watch for. Satan's original aim, his planned mark of the beast to seal the unbeliever, is now in the works.

Invasion from Above and Below

We have seen in the previous chapters how we as believers are involved in a battle against the powers of darkness. We are admonished to stand against them. How? We confess that Jesus Christ is Lord; He is the eternal Victor over all the powers of darkness. When we live in such a fashion, the evil one cannot touch us, even though we are sinners by nature.

Remember, as sinners by nature, the devil has a legal right to accuse us before God. That is what we read in Revelation 12:10: "...the accuser of our brethren is cast down, which accused them before our God day and night." He rightfully does so because whenever we sin, we are in Lucifer's territory. That is the problem we are faced with all the days of our life here on earth.

But as is evident from that verse, the accuser is now cast down. Why? Because the saints at that moment are raptured into heaven; thus, the devil lost his legitimate and rightful job to be the accuser in heaven once and for all. That is the point when the world will literally experience hell on earth. The Bible says, "...Woe to the inhabiters of the earth and of the sea! for the devil is come down unto you, having great wrath, because he knoweth that he hath but a short time" (Revelation 12:12).

Incidentally, this devastates the teaching of the so-called Mid and Post-Tribulation Rapture. When the devil comes down on earth, he comes to a place that lies in darkness; there is no more light and no more salt. Satan can have his heyday. Although he is already the god of this world, he still has to fulfill his aim: he wants to seal each individual nonbeliever with the mark of the beast for eternal damnation.

Jesus Our Advocate

In the meantime (before the Rapture), we have a lawyer to defend us. He is our advocate: "My little children, these things write I unto you, that ye sin not. And if any man sin, we have an advocate with the Father, Jesus Christ the righteous: and he is the propitiation for our sins: and not for ours only, but also for the sins of the whole world" (1 John 2:1-2). In plain words, Jesus tells the accuser, "I paid for his sins." That is the distinct difference between the world at large and we who believe.

The God of This World

Today, there are 192 UN recognized nations on planet Earth. Among these nations, the Church of Jesus Christ resides. It does not matter whether the nation calls itself Christian, Muslim, Hindu, atheist, or is governed by democracy, socialism, communism, dictatorship, or monarchy—all belong to the world. That is why the Bible admonishes us, "Love not the world, neither the things that are in the world. If any man love the world, the love of the Father is not in him" (1 John 2:15).

The intellectual elite of this world really don't know who put us here, the purpose of our existence, and where we are going.

That fact needs to be understood completely; otherwise, we allow the deceiver to confuse us and we neglect our calling to be light and salt.

The world lies in darkness. They really and truly don't know what is going on. When one reads the statements of the intellectual elite of this world, one immediately realizes that they really don't know who put us here, the purpose of our existence, and where we are going. They don't know because they are in darkness. The Bible says, "...the god of this world hath blinded the minds of them which believe not" (2 Corinthians 4:4). That's a simple fact.

Satan's Real Aim

What is Satan aiming for? One answer: to be worshiped.

Jesus was led by the Spirit into the wilderness to be tempted of the devil. Matthew 4:8-9 reads: "Again, the devil taketh him up into an exceeding high mountain, and sheweth him all the kingdoms of the world, and the glory of them; and saith unto him, All these things will I give thee, if thou wilt fall down and worship me." That is the devil's ultimate aim.

This fact also reveals that there is no such thing as "One nation under God." That is wishful thinking, and does not correspond to the teaching of Holy Scripture. The god of this world, the prince of darkness, the devil showed Jesus "the kingdoms of the world, and the glory of them." Quite obviously, he is the legitimate owner of all people on planet Earth. He says to Jesus, "All these things will I give thee." You can't give something to somebody if you don't own it. The devil is claiming Scripture, "He who sins is of the devil." It simply means all are of the devil. If we don't allow this truth to sink in, we will be quickly led astray by the spirit of nationalism, which is the greatest danger to the Church in our days.

The spirit of nationalism is the greatest danger to the Church in our days.

Paul's Testimony

We do well to take as an example the Apostle Paul. He is called the apostle of the Gentiles. When we read his testimony in Philippians, we note that this man really had reasons to be extremely proud; he could have been a super-nationalist: "Circumcised the eighth day, of the stock of Israel, of the tribe of Benjamin, an Hebrew of the Hebrews; as touching the law, a Pharisee" (Philippians 3:5). Then he adds in verse 6: "...touching the righteousness which is in the law, blameless." I don't think any of us can match the Apostle Paul, yet when it comes to his position in Jesus Christ, he has something shocking to say: "Yea doubtless, and I count all things but loss for the excellency of the knowledge of Christ Jesus my Lord: for whom I have suffered the loss of all things, and do count them but dung, that I may win Christ" (verse 8). My very best, the thing I admire, the reason for my pride is "but dung." My nation, my heritage, my national anthem, I myself "but dung"?

This should teach us to realize our position in Jesus Christ our Lord; in comparison, any earthly citizenship is "but dung." That, however, does not mean we should be disrespectful toward our country and our government; we give honor to whom honor is due. We respect all authority, as instructed in Romans chapter 13 and 1 Peter 2.

Sealing Unbelievers with the Mark of the Beast

But there is more: while the devil controls humanity because he has the legitimate right to every soul on planet Earth, he desires to go one step further. He wants to be worshiped by all of humanity. That is his goal. The devil wants to mimic the victory of Jesus; he plans to fulfill Bible prophecy, such as Philippians 2:10-11: "That at the name of Jesus every knee should bow, of things in heaven, and things in earth, and things under the earth; and that every tongue should confess that Jesus Christ is Lord, to the glory of God the Father."

Worshiping the image of the beast and receiving the mark of the beast is the seal of Satan; you are doomed for eternity.

That means, all on earth must bow their knees to Antichrist, and it will happen.

Worshiping the Image

We know from Scripture that the devil will be successful; all people on earth will worship him. That is what it says in Revelation 13:8: "And all that dwell upon the earth shall worship him...." In order to accomplish this, the false prophet will cause the people on earth to build an image of the beast, and that image must be worshiped. The Bible says, "...as many as would not worship the image of the beast should be killed" (Revelation 13:15).

Worshiping the image of the beast and receiving the mark of the beast is the seal of Satan; you are doomed for eternity.

The other seal, the real one, is the sign of the Holy Spirit. Ephesians 1:13 says, "In whom ye also trusted, after that ye heard the word of truth, the gospel of your salvation: in whom also after that ye believed, ye were sealed with that holy Spirit of promise."

Original Challenge

The prophet Isaiah shows us the origin of sin: "How art thou fallen from heaven, O Lucifer, son of the morning! how art thou cut down to the ground, which didst weaken the nations! For thou hast said in thine heart, I will ascend into heaven, I will exalt my throne above the stars of God: I will sit also upon the mount of the congregation, in the sides of the north: I will ascend above the heights of the clouds; I will be like the most High" (Isaiah 14:12-14).

Note the "I will" of Lucifer, particularly the last sentence, "I will be like the most High." That is his goal; he is the father of lies, the murderer from the beginning. He has successfully placed all of humanity under his authority because of sin—"He who sins is of the devil."

There is only one escape: through Jesus Christ our Lord, who poured out His blood on Calvary's Cross to pay for the sins of each sinner in the entire world.

Next, we will see the progress of the world under the inspiration of Satan.

CHAPTER 14

ECONOMIC, POLITICAL AND RELIGIOUS DIVERSITY

Virtually all nations of the world exhibit the slogan, "United we stand, divided we fall." But the new form of globalism could be summarized, "Divided we stand, united we fall." That, in brief, will be the end of human civilization as we know it.

Global Diversity of the Church

Christians are a diverse group: they speak hundreds, if not thousands of different languages, are geographically separated by oceans, rivers, mountains, and deserts, and have different cultures, traditions and holidays. While the Church is diverse here on earth, it is one in the spiritual realm. The Church is perfectly united in our Lord: "For our conversation is in heaven; from whence also we look for the Saviour, the Lord Jesus Christ" (Philippians 3:20).

What About the Ecumenical Movement?

The goal of the Ecumenical Movement is to unite the various Christian denominations into one global church. Logically, this sounds good. Why should we fight each other? Why not have a unified organization, able to effectively influence the world at large? But, there is something very wrong with such an argument. The Church of Jesus Christ, consisting of all truly born-again believers, cannot be identified with an organizational infrastructure. The attempt to create a visible manifestation of the Church on earth is something that man cannot do. Why not? Because God has already done so.

The True Church Is Truly One

We often hear much lamenting about the deplorable condition of the Church: there is strife, divisiveness, disagreement, and sometimes even outright fights occur within certain denominations and local churches. That however, is nothing new. Paul writes to the Corinthians, "...lest there be debates, envyings, wraths, strifes, backbitings, whisperings, swellings, tumults" (2 Corinthians 12:20). Those reprehensible things are unfortunately often the case outwardly. But the true Church of Jesus Christ, without any organizational infrastructure, is already perfectly one in Christ.

Jesus' prayer clearly demonstrates that perfect unity of the Church already exists, "And the glory which thou gavest me I have given them; that they may be one, even as we are one: I in them, and thou in me, that they may be made perfect in one; and that the world may know that thou hast sent me, and hast loved them, as thou hast loved me" (John 17:22-23). In the world we may have disagreements, but in Christ Jesus we are perfectly one.

In plain language, don't fix something that isn't broken.

Extreme Diversity of the Nations

We already mentioned that the United Nations has recognized around 192 nations. However, that does not constitute the end of diversity, because many of these nations are divided into innumerable ethnic groups, tribes, family clans, etc.

We should also realize that some of these various groups have an ancient history with traditions and cultures going back thousands of years.

That is one of the problems that the Western nations have overlooked when dealing with southern Asia, the Middle East, and Africa.

Even to this day, we hear of the Afghan problem, which the West simply tries to resolve as a political issue, but it is actually much more complicated. Long before there was a United States of America, the tribes in Afghanistan had their own territory, leadership, language, culture, and tradition.

When we look at the Middle East, it's a similar story; although some players are ancient nations such as Egypt, Libya, Syria, Persia (Iran), and Babylon (Iraq), the territory of these nations was often haphazardly determined by European colonial powers. That's just one of the many reasons the conflict continues. So, how is the devil going to fix this seemingly unresolvable problem?

Three Important Things Must Happen

In order for these nations to cooperate with one another and with the so-called Western powers, there has to be 1. economic uniformity, 2. political uniformity, and finally, 3. religious uniformity.

We will address each of these topics individually.

1. Global Economy

The world's economic system is actually leading the way. Globalism is a reality, and no nation or corporation of significance can exist without being a member of the global family. As a participating member nation, one has to adhere to various laws, rules, and regulations. That may not be easy, but it is being done. That's the foundation our modern economic society is built upon.

For example: Nestle is the world's largest food distributor, operating in most countries of the world. But only a few actually know that it is a Swiss company, founded in 1866 by Henri Nestle of Vevey, Switzerland, where their headquarters is located. The company is so globalized that the national origin has become insignificant.

The most successful integration of diverse nations has been accomplished by the European Union.

From the relatively insignificant Coal and Steel Treaty signed in 1957 in Rome, the EU has developed into the world's largest economy. They have become the world's greatest importers and exporters.

The uniqueness of the Union consists of the fact that the present (2011) 27 member nations retain their identity as sovereign nations. Language, culture, tradition, custom, and even holidays are recognized and respected throughout the Union. Their motto is, "United in Diversity." That slogan opens the door for the rest of the world to follow.

2. Political Diversity

As mentioned, democracy is the most popular

form of government the world over, although there is noticeable diversity among the various democracies.

The level of freedom is often expressed in the diversity of political parties. For example, Israel's election in 2009 ended with 13 different parties being elected to occupy the 120 seats in the Parliament. From those 13 different parties, a coalition had to be formed to create a functioning government. Another 21 parties were also running in the election, but did not win a seat.

A similar pattern can be seen in Europe, where governments can only be formed by a coalition of various parties in order to make up a required majority. As a large country, only the United States is left with a two-party system; subsequently, this form of government has little future.

In the Middle East, the only functioning democratic government is Israel. Lebanon may come in second place, but is presently very unstable. Elections throughout the Arab world are more or less determined by a one-party system, led by a coalition of rulers or outright dictators.

3. Religious Diversity

It seems all but impossible for the world's religions to unify. Although many movements and a number of political figures and celebrities are working feverishly to create a one-world religion, it is our understanding that such is not necessary. After all, Muslims will not become Christians, neither will Catholics become Protestants. Most of them would rather die than change, so how can Revelation 13:8 be fulfilled, "And all that dwell upon the earth shall worship him"? Here again we find the answer in the motto, "United in Diversity."

Example: Nebuchadnezzar's Image

Daniel chapter 3 records how the world ruler King Nebuchadnezzar of Babylon attempted to create a one-world religion, but failed in the end.

Here is the story: "Nebuchadnezzar the king made an image of gold, whose height was threescore cubits, and the breadth thereof six cubits: he set it up in the plain of Dura, in the province of Babylon." That must have been a very impressive image, at approximately 27 meters (90 feet) high, making it as high as a six to seven story building;

nothing had ever been seen like it in splendor and glory.

Worship the Image—Compulsory

Then King Nebuchadnezzar causes his political leaders, financial treasurers, law enforcement officers, and all the heads of his provinces to meet in the Valley of Dura. What was the purpose? "Then an herald cried aloud, To you it is commanded, O people, nations, and languages, That at what time ye hear the sound of the cornet, flute, harp, sackbut, psaltery, dulcimer, and all kinds of musick, ye fall down and worship the golden image that Nebuchadnezzar the king hath set up: and whoso falleth not down and worshippeth shall the same hour be cast into the midst of a burning fiery furnace" (Daniel 3:4-6).

There was no requirement to change one's religion, to disregard one's idols. In modern language, they could all remain Catholics or Protestants, Muslims or Hindus, atheists or agnostics. They only had to do one thing, "fall down and worship the golden image that Nebuchadnezzar the king had set up."

People may retain their religion, tradition, identity, language, culture, etc., but one thing must be done, and that is worship the image. Thus it will be in the final days of the end times when a man-made image is to be worshiped—and if not? "...Cause that as many as would not worship the image of the beast should be killed."

Three Jews Oppose

During Daniel's time, we read of three young Jews who refused to worship the image Nebuchadnezzar had set up. As a result, they were thrown into the prepared fiery furnace. But as we know, they came out unsinged because God intervened supernaturally:

"Then Nebuchadnezzar came near to the mouth of the burning fiery furnace, and spake, and said, Shadrach, Meshach, and Abednego, ye servants of the most high God, come forth, and come hither. Then Shadrach, Meshach, and Abednego, came forth of the midst of the fire. And the princes, governors, and captains, and the king's counsellors, being gathered together, saw these men, upon whose bodies the fire had no power, nor was an hair of their head singed, neither were their coats changed, nor the smell of fire had passed on them"

(Daniel 3:26-27).

As a result of these three Jewish men holding fast to the God of Israel, Nebuchadnezzar institutionalized respect and honor for the God of Israel: "Therefore I make a decree, That every people, nation, and language, which speak any thing amiss against the God of Shadrach, Meshach, and Abednego, shall be cut in pieces, and their houses shall be made a dunghill: because there is no other God that can deliver after this sort" (verse 29).

Satan, the Lord of Sinners

We must emphasize again that the Arab Revolution was and is not caused by an outside force such as a foreign country. If we were to follow that theory, we would then ignore fulfillment of prophecy. After all, the god of this world is in charge; that's a Biblical fact. He is the originator of the upheaval of the nations.

Satan is the cause of sin and the lord of all sinners. He is the one who incited Cain to kill his brother Abel. From that point on, innumerable wars have been fought and millions upon millions of people have been killed. That continues until this very day.

Jesus prophesied that such would be the case when He said, "And ye shall hear of wars and rumours of wars: see that ye be not troubled: for all these things must come to pass, but the end is not yet. For nation shall rise against nation, and kingdom against kingdom: and there shall be famines, and pestilences, and earthquakes, in divers places" (Matthew 24:6-7).

More Earthquakes?

Speaking of earthquakes, the media reported in detail about the 9.0 Richter scale earthquake in Japan on 11 March 2011, resulting in a tsunami which took the lives of thousands, destroyed industries, dwelling places, and worse, caused havoc at a nuclear power station. This was the largest earthquake recorded in Japan since records were kept some 140 years ago. The question often asked is, is there an increase in earthquakes?

Here are the facts concerning earthquakes:

> Earthquakes, worldwide for 2002-2011 are published by the U.S. Geological Survey National Earthquake Information Center as follows:

Number of Earthquakes Worldwide for 2000 - 2011 [31]

Magnitude	2000	2001	2002	2003	2004	2005	2006	2007	2008	2009	2010	2011
8.0 to 9.9	1	1	0	1	2	1	2	4	0	1	1	1
7.0 to 7.9	14	15	13	14	14	10	9	14	12	16	21	7
6.0 to 6.9	146	121	127	140	141	140	142	178	168	144	151	80
5.0 to 5.9	1344	1224	1201	1203	1515	1693	1712	2074	1768	1895	1944	764
4.0 to 4.9	8008	7991	8541	8462	10888	13917	12838	12078	12291	6801	10402	2445
3.0 to 3.9	4827	6266	7068	7624	7932	9191	9990	9889	11735	2903	4312	382
2.0 to 2.9	3765	4164	6419	7727	6316	4636	4027	3597	3860	3015	4580	544
1.0 to 1.9	1026	944	1137	2506	1344	26	18	42	21	26	37	2
0.1 to 0.9	5	1	10	134	103	0	2	2	0	1	0	0

This should settle the question regarding increased earthquakes.

We need to learn not to read something into the Bible that is not written. Jesus does not say there will be more wars and rumors of wars, neither does He say there will be more pestilences and earthquakes.

These horrible catastrophes such as in Japan, however, remind us that God is in charge, that man is just a little speck of dust and is totally dependent upon the Creator and not on the creation.

Earthquakes, tsunamis, hurricanes, tornados, etc. are called natural catastrophes, but as we already mentioned, they are in the hands of God who is the Creator of all things.

Satan's Great Wonders

Having said that, we realize that Satan, the great imitator, must demonstrate to the people of the world that he is in control of nature as well. Thus, we read about the false prophet, beast number two in Revelation 13:13, "And he doeth great wonders, so that he maketh fire come down from heaven on the earth in the sight of men." At this point in time, we have seen no one come forward demonstrating supernatural signs to the world. But, it will happen; it's simply yet to be fulfilled.

Satan Must Make Peace

The devil, also called the great dragon, the old serpent and Satan, cannot attain the position of being worshiped if he continues to incite nation against nation. That is why the nations of the world, under the authority of the god of this world, must produce convincing peace on planet Earth. That's part of democracy invading Islam.

There is definitely going to be peace on earth, and this type of peace will be accomplished through deception. Doubtless, democracy is going to be a major contributing factor toward achieving that peace.

Daniel's Prophecy

Just a few verses from Daniel chapter 11 should help: "And in his estate shall stand up a vile person, to whom they shall not give the honour of the kingdom: but he shall come in peaceably, and obtain the kingdom by flatteries. And with the arms of a flood shall they be overflown from before him, and shall be broken; yea, also the prince of the covenant. And after the league made with him he shall work deceitfully: for he shall come up, and shall become strong with a small people" (verses 21-23). Note the words "peaceably...flatteries...deceitfully."

Political Democracy

It does not matter what our political preference may be; public office can only be obtained if the candidate makes use of the two words in particular, "peaceable" and "flatteries." We also will agree that it makes no difference whether these peaceable flatteries are true or not. Even if the words are deceitful, most voters have made up their mind because of party platforms. After a candidate has won the office, he is no longer obligated to fulfill his promises. That is the path to becoming a leader, elected by the votes of the people under democracy.

Now we should understand that the world's last government is the worst, while the dictatorial government of Nebuchadnezzar is called the best. Democratically elected candidates can change their laws (promises); Nebuchadnezzar could not.

Antichrist Revealed

Daniel reveals the Antichrist in chapter 11. His character and attitude is identified in verses 36-37: "And the king shall do according to his will; and he shall exalt himself, and magnify himself above every god, and shall speak marvellous things against the God of gods, and shall prosper till the indignation be accomplished: for that that is determined shall be done. Neither shall he regard the God of his fathers, nor the desire of women, nor regard any god: for he shall magnify himself above all." Self exaltation is a mark of Lucifer, "...I will be like the most high" (Isaiah 14:15), which is also the mark of the Antichrist, "Who opposeth and exalteth himself above all that is called God, or that is worshipped; so that he as God sitteth in the temple of God, shewing himself that he is God" (2

Thessalonians 2:4). That is the man who will bring peace to earth, although only temporarily.

The Only Real Peace

Jesus stated, "Peace I leave with you, my peace I give unto you: not as the world giveth, give I unto you. Let not your heart be troubled, neither let it be afraid" (John 14:27). That's real peace, not to be confused with any other type of peace on earth.

Any and all peace treaties of the past, the present, and the future serve only one goal: the establishment of global peace under the authority of Antichrist.

Never must we degrade the peace our Lord gives to us with the peace and freedom politicians and nationalists tell us about. Peace, real, genuine peace, cannot be established in any way, shape, or form except through the Prince of Peace. His death on the cross condemned sin in the flesh. True peace comes only by death. That is why the Apostle Paul so emphatically stated, "For I determine not to know anything among you, save Jesus Christ, and him crucified" (1 Corinthians 2:2).

For the devil to present the Antichrist as the Messiah to the world, he has to create peace on earth. Therefore, any and all peace treaties of the past, the present, and the future serve only one goal: the establishment of global peace under the authority of Antichrist.

In order for this global peace to be established, the Arab world must be integrated. They must attain political, financial and economic power for the people. Read on to learn "why Arab nations were left out."

CHAPTER 15

WHY ARAB NATIONS WERE LEFT OUT

When analyzing the Arab nations, we are dealing with history dating back to Abraham's time. The Arab world had seen its glory days, but then a decline. Today, the potential of being put back onto the pedestal of the world scene requires a drastic change—and that, the author believes, is expressed by the pro-democracy movements.

The Arab Oil the West Needs

> *With the advent of the communication explosion, the Arab people realized more than ever that they are not participating in the success and prosperity of the modern world.*

The Arabs are the possessors of vast stores of the world's energy, yet the general population is not benefiting from these riches. In plain words, the Muslim world missed out on the Industrial Revolution. Although they supply the oil and use the money to buy merchandise and equipment from the EU, Asia, and America, the people are left in poverty. The Arabs are aware that the industrialized nations are dependent upon their natural resources. To secure those resources, Europe and the United States directly and indirectly supported dictators throughout the Arab world. That's a fact the Arabs have not forgotten, and will not in the future.

With the advent of the communication explosion, the Arab people realized more than ever that they are not participating in the success and prosperity of the modern world. The cars they drive are imported from Europe or Japan. Trucks and buses mostly come from Europe. Communication technology and related hardware are imported from the USA.

Except for crude oil and petroleum products such as textiles and chemicals, the Arab world has little to offer. They have not attained a significant place in the industrial world. The rich were getting richer and the poor were languishing in their misery and poverty.

Those are some of the reasons why the people decided to revolt against their leaders. With the internet, satellite, radio, and television, the masses of the people realized that their dictatorial governments were the cause for being left out. That was one of the contributing causes for the rebellion against their governments.

What Does the Bible Say About the Arabs?

From Genesis 17, we know that Ishmael was Abraham's firstborn, but he was not the son of Sarah. Nevertheless, there is a promise given by God, "And as for Ishmael, I have heard thee: Behold, I have blessed him, and will make him fruitful, and will multiply him exceedingly; twelve princes shall he beget, and I will make him a great nation" (Genesis 17:20). There are various opinions regarding Ishmael and his descendants, but one thing is clear: he was the son of an Egyptian woman called Hagar. So we may call the Arabs the descendants of Ishmael.

We must take notice of the words of God, "I have blessed him...I will make him a great nation." Has that been fulfilled? If yes, then when? Just looking at the numbers relating to global oil reserves, the figures are impressive.

Oil Monopoly

Here is a chart showing where the oil is according to region:[32]

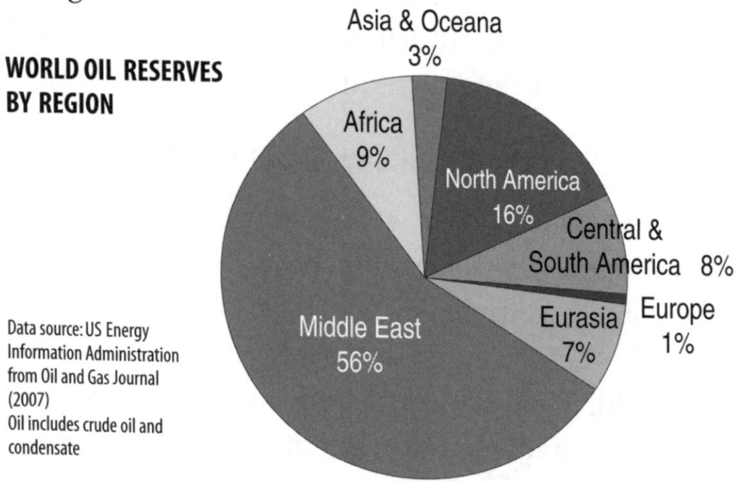

If we consider these statistics, then indeed Ishmael is now and will be "a great nation."

From Leadership to Poverty

Approximately 1,000 years ago, according to history, the Middle East had a larger share of Gross Domestic Product than Europe. An *Economist* article dated 29 January 2011, states that "by 1700 the Middle East's share [world GDP] had fallen to just 2 percent and Europe's had risen to 22 percent." Yet the article also reveals that the Muslim Koran is more business oriented than the Christian New Testament:

> The standard explanations for this decline are all unsatisfactory. One is that the spirit of Islam is hostile to commerce. But if anything Islamic scripture is more pro-business than Christian texts. Muhammad was a merchant, and the Koran is full of praise for commerce.[33]

So, what happened?

New Testament Anti-Business?

The word "poor" appears thirty-five times in the New Testament, and the word "rich" forty times. But in reading these verses, we notice that the poor

So why has the once mighty Muslim camp deteriorated and Europe excelled? The simple answer is, the Arabs did not change.

are never condemned, but the rich are. For example, Jesus said, "But woe unto you that are rich! for ye have received your consolation" (Luke 6:24). Addressing the poor, James writes, "Do not rich men oppress you, and draw you before the judgment seats?" (James 2:6). A strong warning against coveting money is given in 1 Timothy 6:5, "Perverse disputings of men of corrupt minds, and destitute of the truth, supposing that gain is godliness: from such withdraw thyself." In reading the entire New Testament, it is quite evident that striving for riches is not supported in our Bible. Yet, the Muslim Koran encourages business-oriented people.

So why has the once mighty Muslim camp deteriorated and Europe excelled? The simple answer is, the Arabs did not change.

Roman Corporation Laws

The same article then reveals an important truth,

"The Middle East fell behind the West because it failed to produce commercial institutions—most notably joint stock companies—that were capable of mobilizing large quantities of productive resources and enduring over time."[34]

> *The Arab world still lags far behind Europe, with only about 28 percent per capita income in comparison.*

"Europeans inherited the idea of the corporation from Roman law," says the writer. That, obviously, is the key to European success; it is based on Roman principles. Such is the case in virtually all countries of the world today.

Only in recent years have Muslim nations followed in "Roman footsteps" and made progress. Yet the Arab world still lags far behind Europe, with only about 28 percent per capita income in comparison.

Those Arab countries that have adopted Roman principles, have done rather well. Qatar, for example, rose to reach the highest GDP per capita in the world. Others such as the United Arab Emirates, Oman, and Bahrain are beginning to enjoy the fruits of Roman, corporation-based laws. But

> *Fueled by the dream and the desire to participate in the prosperity of Western nations, democracy is the only answer.*

these successful Arab nations allowed Western, capital-intensive business, dominated by Jews and Christians, to opt out of Islamic law, the writer states.

There is no reason to doubt that most of the Arab nations will follow in the footsteps of Rome sooner or later. That is part of progressive democracy.

Islamic Invasion or Democratic Invasion?

While the Islamic religion is a contributing factor in the uprising, based on the various interviews and statements in the media, it is obvious that religion is not the major reason—poverty is.

Most Arabs did not see a likeable model in Iran, becoming an Islamic nation ruled by religion. Even devout Muslims are not in favor of their country being governed by strict and capricious Islamists. Again, the only alternative presenting itself is democracy. Although many favor Islamic guidance or supervision, they do not prefer Islamic rulership.

Democracy, they realize, no matter what type,

will at least give them some power to influence their government. Fueled by the dream and the desire to participate in the prosperity of Western nations, democracy is the only answer.

Change or Perish

Although great progress has been made in many Arab countries in the past several decades, it is obviously not sufficient to appease the population at large. Even though the improvement is significant, life in the industrial world went ahead at a faster speed, thus creating more space between the Arabs and the European world (West).

Regardless of the immediate outcome within the Arab League, the long-term tendency will prove democracy's invasion of Islam.

There is enough reason to believe that the Arab world will be energized in the not too distant future. But the question still lingers, how will the West accommodate the rise of the Arab nations? We believe the answer lies in Europe's motto, "United in Diversity." The Arab nations will not be transformed into Europeans, but will become a significant power within the family of nations. The oil will be the lubricant toward prosperity.

CHAPTER 16

THE MASTER DECEIVER AT HIS BEST

While the world scene may look like uncontrolled chaos, it is a mistake to think so. In the midst of all the confusion, revolutions, and upheavals, Satan follows a very distinct plan to bring the masses of the people under his absolute control.

The prince of darkness has to offer the world something everyone can agree on.

"Nations of the World, Unite"

Realizing all the commotion that is going on in the world, and being aware of the often extreme disunity among the nations, particularly in the Arab world, the question arises, how will the god of this world unite humanity? The answer is simple: deception. That means the prince of darkness has to offer the world something everyone can agree on.

What do people want? ALL people the world over want peace, security, and prosperity. ALL want to make this world a better place to live. That is the criteria on which ALL political, economic and religious systems are built. Improving mankind, creating cooperation between all people, with certain guarantees of peace, prosperity and security embody the desire and dream of mankind. The only question remaining is how to bring this about.

According to Bible prophecy, it will happen. The majority of the world population will enthusiastically welcome this new peaceful global system, led by one man who will present himself to be the savior of the world. The Bible says, "And all the world wondered after the beast."

This is not going to be a national event limited to one country or two, but will literally be global, "all the world."

Antichrist on the Way

We are not sure about the exact timing of the appearance of the Antichrist, but we do know that the final preparations are being made today. There are many contributing factors pointing to the soon coming fulfillment.

The most significant sign of the end times is the reappearance of the Jewish nation in the land of Israel.

The most significant sign of the end times is the reappearance of the Jewish nation in the land of Israel, which today is contested by all nations of the world without exception.

Some may object and say Israel has many friends. The United States, for example, is a great ally and supporter of the nation of Israel. That cannot be denied. However, neither can we deny that the support of Israel is politically motivated. The reason we can state that all nations, including the USA, oppose Israel is due to the fact that not one agrees to the geographical borders given by God to Abraham, "from the river of Egypt unto the great river, the river Euphrates." That means in reality, "anti-Israel" is equal to "anti-God."

No politician or head of state in their right mind would declare that such are the borders of the land of Israel. The truth is, all nations vehemently oppose Israel's possession of the Promised Land. Therefore, God's judgment will be executed upon all nations, "I will also gather all nations, and will bring them down into the valley of Jehoshaphat, and will plead with them there for my people and for my heritage Israel, whom they have scattered among the nations, and parted my land" (Joel 3:2).

Only One Master

The Church is different; she is the light of the world and salt on earth. We are the ambassadors of truth. Jesus said, "My sheep hear my voice, and I know them, and they follow me" (John 10:27).

When we meddle in Lucifer's territory, we become partial and fight for political preference.

This is a mighty truth but a strong warning to each of us: stay with the flock so you will hear His voice and follow Him. Those who separate themselves and get entangled in the affairs of this world, will be less and less able to hear His voice. When we meddle in Lucifer's territory, we become partial and fight for political preference, thereby becoming involved in their agenda. Finally, we lose our God-given authority to be light and salt.

Many dear Christians have lost their testimony and subsequent calling because they went after those things that belong to the world. Although it may seem noble and morally upright, and our motives pure and clean, we can only serve one Lord: "No man can serve two masters: for either he will hate the one, and love the other; or else he will hold to the one, and despise the other..." (Matthew 6:24).

There are no two ways about it, no possibility of mixing these two issues—either I am for the Lord or for the world. The Christian's allegiance is clear. We are passing through this earth on our way to eternity, and have only one calling and one Master to follow: Jesus Christ our Savior. He is the only representative for us before the throne of God.

Separating God and Country

This is a difficult issue. After all, we live in this world, have duties and responsibilities, and naturally, we love our family and our country, but the issue is not to confuse these two diametrically opposed realities. We are in the world but not of the world. That must be a reality in our life.

> *Often, we hear the slogan, "God and country." That is a dangerous statement. It is based on the assumption that these things belong together.*

Often, we hear the slogan, "God and country." That is a dangerous statement. It is based on the assumption that these things belong together; however, they do not. I am 100 percent for God and I am 100 percent for my country, but never for "God and country." To keep this strict separation will prevent us from falling. We can only stand against the prince of darkness if we are not mingling in his territory.

The Dragon's Victory March

The world will yet experience the seemingly glorious unity of all nations on planet Earth. They will enjoy the success of the new one world government. Peace and prosperity will have been achieved, and the people will shout, "Peace, peace."

> *The world will yet experience the seemingly glorious unity of all nations on planet Earth.*

In the not too distant future, Revelation 13:3-4 will be fulfilled: "And I saw one of his heads as it were wounded to death; and his deadly wound was healed: and all the world wondered after the beast. And they worshipped the dragon which gave power unto the beast: and they worshipped the beast, saying, Who is like unto the beast? who is able to make war with him?"

They are not only praising and applauding this great man, but it actually says they "worshipped the dragon" and "worshipped the beast." This seems virtually unbelievable, but it is true because it is written so in Holy Scripture.

That is also the future of the Islamic world. They are not exempt when it says all the world, for this includes all the religions as well.

Right now, there are different organizations and movements feverishly working toward unifying the world's religions. They will fail in doing so as we already mentioned; people are unlikely to change their religion, and some would rather die than change, but the spirit of uniting the world's religions, this global ecumenical movement will find its answer in the appearance of the Antichrist.

Hero/Idol Worship

Can we really expect the whole world to worship a man? The answer is yes. Just think for a moment about the position of celebrities, politicians, actors, or sports heroes; people will pay exorbitant amounts of money in order to identify with these hero-idols. When a sports hero recommends a certain pair of tennis shoes, millions of people will actually go out and buy the product. Why? Because their hero/idol has commanded them to do so.

Someone may now object, "I would not do it."

That may be so, but facts prove otherwise. Merchandisers pay millions of dollars to celebrities for them to endorse their product—for good reason.

Many of us underestimate the power of public relations. We may think, "It doesn't affect me," but facts, figures, and hard cash in the pockets of the merchandisers prove that cleverly designed promotions leverage great influence on the minds of the people.

The $3 Baseball Cap

This may sound insignificant, but I think it is worth mentioning. Not too long ago, I went to a store to buy a baseball cap. Virtually all of them had some logo imprinted, advertising a certain brand or a sports club. They sold for around 10-12 dollars. Looking at the bottom shelf, I found what I was looking for—caps with no advertising. They sold for $3. Logical thinking would conclude that if I wear a baseball cap with a certain logo, I am promoting that product and should get paid, or at least pay less for the item. Why would I pay extra money just to endorse a company? Yet, that is actually what millions, even hundreds of millions of people do on the daily basis. They are "worshiping" a product, a brand, an image. They gladly and willingly pay extra just to support this hero-idol without getting any benefits for it. That is part of hero/idol worship.

Failed Propaganda

We already mentioned Soviet communism. Why did they fail? They did not promote profit. Way too much energy was spent on political promotion. Yet, they failed to use suitable propaganda for their products. They were convinced that product advertising was a waste of time and resources. That was the beginning of the end of Soviet communism.

Failure to Change

Another important item contributing to the demise of Soviet communism was the inability to change. Karl Marx and his work *Das Kapital* was the Soviet Bible, relating to Europe's condition in 1800, published in 1867. Karl Marx and contributing editor Friedrich Engels released an extensive treatise on political economy, applicable for those days. The economy was primarily based on agriculture, and the Industrial Revolution had barely begun. Yet when the Soviet Union was established in about 1922, Marx's *Das Kapital* was already outdated. Nevertheless, Soviet communism fiercely defended and enforced Marxism nevertheless. Even after recognizing that Marxism no longer works in the 20th century, the Soviets used force to forbid their citizens from traveling abroad. That's the worst-case scenario for any nation. By limiting travel and not allowing intellectual freedom and interchange, isolationism followed, resulting in the drying up of fresh sources of science and technology. Their own technological know-how became obsolete and stale. In plain words, Soviet communism perished because they refused to change.

Will Nationalism Change?

All nations have their political, military and sports icons. They all drape their heroes and idols in their country's flag, always being partial, always leading their citizens to believe, "My nation is the greatest." That, incidentally, is not an American invention, but has been practiced throughout history by all the nations of the world.

Only when we begin to read the Bible without prejudice will we see that "the whole world lieth in wickedness." We as Christians live "in the midst of a crooked and perverse nation," and the reality that we have been delivered "from this present evil world." These Scriptures should cause us to wake up and realize what a horrendous insult any type of national pride is to our true heavenly citizenship and our Lord Jesus Christ.

Global Entertainment Contributing to Change

The entertainment industry has already bridged the gap between nations. Film stars, for example, are "worshiped" in many different nations in the world. The entertainment industry, particularly modern music, is leading the world toward increasing unity.

In olden days, it was classical music that bridged the gap between the diverse nations. But it was reserved only for the elite who were able to attend live performances of great artists, particularly throughout Europe. Today, with the communication explosion, all has changed: music can be bought for a relatively small amount and taken home or enjoyed virtually anywhere—in the car, on a plane, or while exercising. This new type of music has not only successfully penetrated the entire world, but is contributing to its unification.

It's been years since we toured Egypt, but I still remember that in the narrow bazaars of Cairo, one could hear virtually any type of Western music. "I'm Dreaming of a White Christmas" is just as popular in the Muslim world as anywhere.

The Great Global Change

Think what would happen if an international figure, whom the world loves and adores, arose to lead the world, promising peace and stability for all. People would bow down and worship such a person.

In Revelation 17 and 18, we are introduced to an identity called Mystery Babylon. In verse 2, we read, "With whom the kings of the earth have committed fornication, and the inhabitants of the earth have been made drunk with the wine of her fornication."

The "kings" in our days are the prime ministers, chancellors, presidents, and political leaders of the nations "of the earth."

What do they do? They "have committed forni-

The whole world is marching toward global unity, intoxicated by its success.

cation," and the world "is made drunk with the wine of her fornication." This is not physical human fornication, but political, financial and economic fornication.

The whole world is marching toward global unity, intoxicated by its success. The powers of darkness are busy transforming sinners into worshipers of Satan. That is the devil's goal. His aim is to seal every person on planet Earth with the mark of the beast, thereby challenging God with the statement, "He/she is mine, eternally doomed!"

The Wine of Fornication

In order for the devil to cause the earth to be "made drunk with the wine of her fornication," he must bring the nations of the world closer together. The Arab world under the leadership of dictators will change, and must be brought into the camp of people-power democracy.

In Revelation 18 verse 3, we read: "For all nations have drunk of the wine of the wrath of her fornication, and the kings of the earth have committed fornication with her, and the merchants of the earth are waxed rich through the abundance of her delicacies." Again, note the words, "all nations...kings of the earth...merchants of the earth...rich through the abundance of her delicacies." That is global success.

The world's political, economic, and financial leaders will have finally solved the world's problems. Now they are celebrating.

The Arab world under the leadership of dictators will change, and must be brought into the camp of people-power democracy.

Global Super Success

Let us read just a few more verses to reemphasize the extreme success, but also the absolute desolation:

"And the kings of the earth, who have committed fornication and lived deliciously with her, shall bewail her, and lament for her, when they shall see the smoke of her burning...The merchants of these things, which were made rich by her, shall stand afar off for the fear of her torment, weeping and wailing...And they cast dust on their heads, and cried, weeping and wailing, saying, Alas, alas, that great city, wherein were made rich all that had ships in the sea by reason of her costliness! for in one hour is she made desolate...And the light of a candle shall shine no more at all in thee; and the voice of the bridegroom and of the bride shall be heard no more at all in thee: for thy merchants were the great men of the earth; for by thy sorceries were all nations deceived" (Revelation 18:9, 15, 19, 23). That is global super success; it is the victory of Satan over all of planet Earth. But let it be said, it is Satan's last victory.

How Close Are We?

> *The fulfillment of global peace will doubtless be under democracy.*

Now the important question, how will the world reach this point of success? When will all the nations of the world cooperate with one another, live in peace and security, and enjoy the labor of their hands? When will they live free of the fear of crime and poverty? The fulfillment of global peace will doubtless be under democracy.

But it can only take place when the light of this world is taken out of the way, when the salt has been removed from planet Earth, when the Church of Jesus Christ is raptured into the presence of the Lord.

Make no mistake, the address of the Church of Jesus Christ is not the United States of America.

The Rapture of the Church

That will be the moment when something mysterious will take place. Suddenly, the Church of Jesus Christ will be removed. This global event will cause the nations of the world to forget their differences. The true Church, in which the Holy Spirit dwells, is the actual hindrance for the development of the spirit of Antichrist. But now, without warning, they have disappeared.

However, the largest bulk of Churchianity will still be present on earth. It is possible that church attendance will shoot up because of the numbers of people mysteriously missing.

Make no mistake, the address of the Church of Jesus Christ is not the United States of America, although church activity and visible manifestation

> *The true Church, consisting only of the believers, is sprinkled all over planet Earth.*

of religion is certainly headquartered here. The true Church, consisting only of the believers, is sprinkled all over planet Earth. We don't know, but it may well be that from the most extreme Muslim nations, where the Church is not permitted to express its activity openly, an unexpectedly large number of true, Bible-believing Christians will be raptured.

Many people from Muslim, Hindu, Buddhist, as well as atheist countries will disappear. That urgency will definitely cause the nations to come closer together. They will be shocked, realizing that something out of this world, something supernatural has taken place.

With the disappearance of many people all over the world, the heads of governments will have to cooperate to the fullest extent and thereby open the doors to any and all compromise. That, we believe, will be the time when Satan demonstrates his last victory on planet Earth.

CHAPTER 17

THE SHAKING OF THE ARAB NATIONS

The Communist Revolution began with the slogan, "Workers of the world, unite!" Today, this can be changed to, "Nations of the world, unite!" People the world over desire to be their own master, do their own thing. The great deceiver is successfully blinding the eyes of unbelievers.

Process of Unity in Diversity

We have already seen that the world is uniting financially, economically and religiously. This is not something we need to discuss or research further. Corporations and nations that do not participate in the process of globalization will be left out. The Arab world at large has been left out of the process of industrialization and democratization. But that is changing, as we now see.

Swissair Example

The famous national airline of Switzerland, Swissair, began in 1931. It became one of the most celebrated airlines, receiving many international awards. Often, they were recognized as the best airline in the world. Swissair was called the "Flying Bank" because of its financial stability. It was a national icon, the pride of the Swiss people.

But something was gradually occurring that went virtually unnoticed. The very success of Swissair caused its management to avoid global airline alliances that were forming during those years. Other major airlines saw that cooperation based on code sharing would be beneficial, making them more competitive and more global.

Swissair was not as keen to be part of that vastly expanding global family, so they ignored this trend. When Swissair finally recognized the need for partnership with other airlines, it was too late. Within a short time, Swissair had to do the unthinkable: cease operation. Although the government subsidized the airline, the final end came on 31 March 2002. (It has since been reorganized under the name "Swiss International Airlines" and is part of the Star Alliance.)

This example shows that individualism cannot last. Independence is a thing of the past. Cooperation and interdependency is the key to the future and success.

Globalism and Islam

Without being fully integrated into globalism, countries and corporations cannot remain successful. For the Arab nations, the ancient Greco-Roman democracy is the most important avenue to guarantee progress and success in the global world.

At the time of writing, there is unrest in most of the Arab nations. Some of the governments have fallen; others are unsteady, with experts predicting that they will fall also.

Of particular interest are Israel's neighbors.

Jordan

Map of Jordan[35]

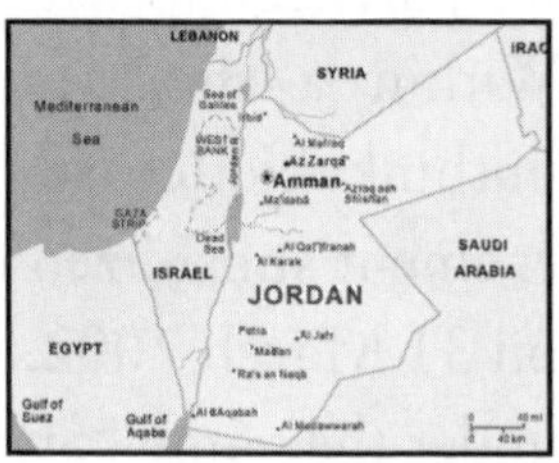

This country is considered to be secure and stable, with a good relationship with the West. Although elections are held periodically, Jordan is ruled by a constitutional monarchy. According to the 2010 Arab Democracy Index, Jordan ranks first when it comes to democratic reforms out of 15 Arab countries.[36] But the news is not all good.

Amnesty International reports:

> Torture and other ill-treatment were reported and at least two men were alleged to have died as a result of police beatings. Thousands of people were held without charge or prospect of trial. Trials before the State Security Court (SSC) continued to breach international standards of fair trial. A new Societies Law opened the way for greater state interference in the work of civil society organizations. Women faced legal and other discrimination and remained inadequately protected against domestic violence; at least 24 were reported to have been victims of so-called honour killings. New regulations improved conditions for migrant domestic workers but still left them vulnerable to exploita-

> tion and abuse. At least 12 people were sentenced to death; there were no executions.[37]

GDP is listed as $5,400 per capita. That is considered dire poverty when compared with its neighbor, Israel, whose GDP for 2010 stood at $29,800.[38]

A large segment of the population is dissatisfied with their conditions; subsequently, Jordan cannot be considered a stable and secure nation.

Lebanon

Map of Lebanon[39]

This country was once called the "Switzerland of the Middle East." Recently, she has barely survived a civil war and is still torn between two major factions: Muslims and Christians (Churchianity). Lebanon can definitely not be called a stable nation. This former French colony is ruled by a parliamentary republic, but is heavily influenced by Syria. The political climate is all but secure. Lebanon's GDP is listed at $14,400 per capita.[40]

Syria

Map of Syria[41]

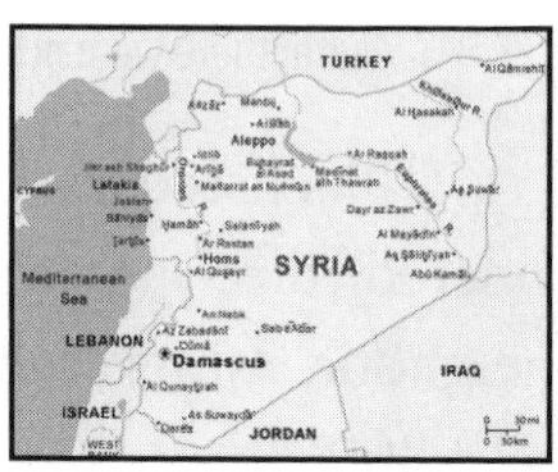

President Bashar al-Assad is a dictator who has followed in his father's footsteps, practicing massive human rights abuses. The nation has continued to operate under emergency law since 1962. Syria is anything but a secure nation. Poverty is definitely an issue, with a per capita GDP of only $4,800.[42]

Egypt

Map of Egypt[43]

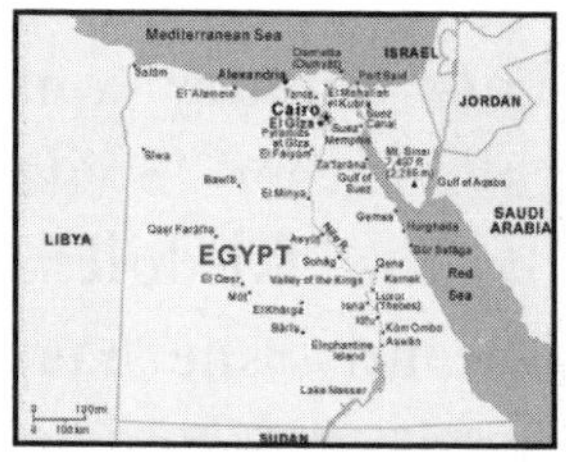

Israel signed a peace treaty with Egypt in 1979. But real peace between these two nations never became a reality. The peace treaty at most could be called a "treaty of tolerance."

Egypt is the largest Arab nation, with approximately 80 million people. Their rebellion against the Hosni Mubarak government has put Egypt on the road to a possible change. But poverty is still a major issue, as the GDP stands at only $6,200 per person.[44]

What will happen when a new government is

voted in remains an unanswered question.

Saudi Arabia

Map of Saudi Arabia[45]

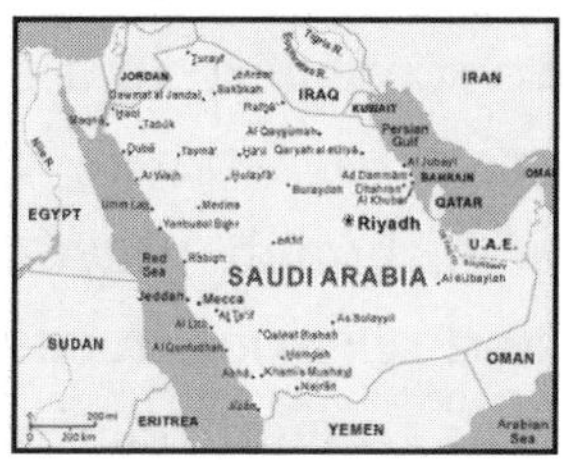

Although this nation does not directly border Israel, it is a very important player in the Arab world. Wikipedia lists its government as an Islamic absolute monarchy. In other words, religious dictatorship or theocracy.

Because of its immense oil reservoir, Saudi Arabia has maintained a close friendship with the West, in particular the United States. Although poverty does not appear to be as big an issue, since the GDP is listed as $24,200,[46] yet this hides the vast inequity between the rich ruling class and the rest of the population.

Saudi Arabia's economy is petroleum based; roughly 80% of budget revenue and 90% of export earnings originate with the oil industry. These immense riches can buy the favor of many people, including much of the population at large, but as economic and political history show, this cannot be sustained indefinitely.

It is noteworthy that the World Economic

Forum listed in their 2010 Global Gender Gap Report, that Saudi Arabia ranked 129th out of 134 countries. Saudi Arabia was the only country to score zero in a category of political empowerment for women.[47]

Although practically ignoring women's rights and religious freedom, Saudi Arabia enjoys excellent foreign relations with most countries, obviously due to oil. Under normal circumstances, Saudi Arabia would be condemned as an oppressive, dictator state by the so-called free world, yet because of oil, all keep silent.

Although practically ignoring women's rights and religious freedom, Saudi Arabia enjoys excellent foreign relations with most countries, obviously due to oil.

Arab Revolution

One thing is becoming overwhelmingly clear: the Arab world wants change, and that change is expressed with one word—democracy. Of course, this is not something that will happen overnight; it will take years to fully implement. But once democracy is established, then the process of integration with the European World (West) will take place.

Muslims and Finance

The world economy is based on borrowing and lending money at interest. That, however, is forbidden in the Koran; subsequently, the Islamic world has been hindered in their participation in European/American style globalism.

The nations who want to participate in the success and prosperity of globalism, must follow the prevailing guideline or be left out.

So far, we have seen there is no second choice, no alternative: the whole world must be integrated into the process of full globalization on all levels of society—politics, economy, finance, and religion.

Not surprisingly, we are seeing the development of contrived "Islamic financing," which is able to skirt the strict prohibitions against earning interest. *The American Prospect* quotes Frank Vogel, an Islamic legal scholar:

> For example, rather than borrowing money to buy some goods, they'll have the bank buy the goods and then resell the goods to the customer, so the bank becomes involved as an owner at one stage of the transaction. That makes it lawful,

> from the Islamic perspective. Whereas if the bank lent the money to the customer, that's an interest-bearing loan, and that's not allowed. So they use slightly different routes, typically involving ownership of goods at some point, to achieve finance.[48]

A *Forbes* article from 2008 says: "There are at least $500 billion worth of Sharia-compliant assets globally, up from just $150 billion a decade ago. But just 20 men (and, yes, they are all men) are the gatekeepers to this lucrative realm."[49]

The Final "Ten Kings"

Finally, we must mention again that the chaotic conditions in the Arab world, and for that matter, anywhere else are caused by demonic powers. Revelation 17:12-13 reveals: "And the ten horns which thou sawest are ten kings, which have received no kingdom as yet; but receive power as kings one hour with the beast. These have one mind, and shall give their power and strength unto the beast."

Although many great Bible scholars have identified the ten kings to be ten nations or ten world power structures, we must question such understanding because of the statement made in the next verse: "These shall make war with the Lamb, and the Lamb shall overcome them." No nation, king, or power structure on earth has the ability to make war against the Lamb. Even if they tried, they could not. Military force—missiles, nuclear bombs, planes, tanks, guns, etc.—is absolutely useless when it comes to making war against the power of heaven.

This reconfirms our repeated insistence that demonic forces are at work. The devil is the king and god of this world; that is a well-established fact. But the devil wants more: he desires to be the savior of world. In order to attain that goal, he must execute his plan to deceive all of mankind. Therefore, the present upheaval in the Arab world is right in line with Satan's aim to bring all nations under his dominion.

Finally, Revelation 13:3-4 and 7-8 will be fulfilled, "And I saw one of his heads as it were wounded to death; and his deadly wound was healed: and all the world wondered after the beast. And they worshipped the dragon which gave power unto the beast: and they worshipped the beast, saying, Who is like unto the beast?

who is able to make war with him?...And it was given unto him to make war with the saints, and to overcome them: and power was given him over all kindreds, and tongues, and nations. And all that dwell upon the earth shall worship him, whose names are not written in the book of life of the Lamb slain from the foundation of the world."

CONCLUSION

Why Do the Heathen Rage?

The Scripture reading from Psalm 2 and the events taking place in the Middle East are the immediate motivating factors for writing this book.

But our enlarged intention is to show that above and beyond any happenings, even the catastrophic earthquake followed by the devastating tsunami in Japan, God remains in control. These events simply serve to fulfill His purpose.

From Daniel 2:44, we learn that the God of heaven is setting up His kingdom, which began with the days of Nebuchadnezzar and continues to this day, climaxing in the establishment of His visible kingdom in the land of Israel, from which He will govern planet Earth.

Parallel to that development, the devil is desperately trying to establish his own kingdom so he can present himself as God, with the targeted aim for the world to worship him.

The Example of Job

To better understand the relationship between God and Satan, let's take a closer look at the man Job.

We begin with the assumption that the reader is Bible literate; he or she knows the book of Job.

This very rich man Job, blessed abundantly of God, is described with the words, "a perfect and an upright man." Then, something strange occurs. The Lord gave authority to Satan, "Behold, all that he has is in thine power; only upon himself put not forth thine hand" (Job 1:12). What next?

Four Devastating Catastrophes

1. "...The Sabeans fell upon them, and took them away; yea, they have slain the servants with the edge of the sword; and I only am escaped alone to tell thee" (Job 1:15). This clearly is manmade, but initiated by Satan.
2. "While he was yet speaking, there came also

> *There is a certain degree of cooperation between God and Satan, but for God's purposes.*

another, and said, The fire of God is fallen from heaven, and hath burned up the sheep, and the servants, and consumed them; and I only am escaped alone to tell thee" (verse 16). Note that it doesn't say, "the fire of Satan," but, "the fire of God is fallen from heaven." Satan receives authority to make use of the fire of God. This is what we call a natural catastrophe, which in reality is supernatural.

3. Next comes another manmade catastrophe: "While he was yet speaking, there came also another, and said, The Chaldeans made out three bands, and fell upon the camels, and have carried them away, yea, and slain the servants with the edge of the sword; and I only am escaped alone to tell thee" (verse 17). Job lost his livestock and his servants. But that's not all; again, we see a supernatural catastrophe:

4. "And, behold, there came a great wind from the wilderness, and smote the four corners of the house, and it fell upon the young men, and they

are dead; and I only am escaped alone to tell thee" (verse 19).

Job lost everything—his livestock and servants, and now worst of all, his seven sons and three daughters. What a horrible catastrophe it must have been for this man. But how does he react? "...the LORD gave, and the LORD hath taken away; blessed be the name of the LORD" (verse 21).

This teaches us that there is a certain degree of cooperation between God and Satan, but for God's purposes.

As believers, we must recognize that God is above and beyond anything that may occur on earth or in heaven.

Identification Crisis

One of the most difficult tasks for any Bible student or scholar is to differentiate between who does what. We have just read that Satan, the enemy of God, used "the fire of God from heaven" to destroy Job's sheep.

As believers, we must recognize that God is above and beyond anything that may occur on earth or in heaven.

Amos, the prophet, summarizes God's actions, "Shall a trumpet be blown in the city, and the people not be afraid? shall there be evil in a city, and the LORD hath not done it?" (Amos 3:6).

So, Why Do the Heathen Rage?

> *It would be a grave mistake to apply the rage to the Arab people only.*

We already mentioned it briefly, but to get a full picture, let us read the first six verses of Psalm 2:

"Why do the heathen rage, and the people imagine a vain thing? The kings of the earth set themselves, and the rulers take counsel together, against the LORD, and against his anointed, saying, Let us break their bands asunder, and cast away their cords from us. He that sitteth in the heavens shall laugh: the Lord shall have them in derision. Then shall he speak unto them in his wrath, and vex them in his sore displeasure. Yet have I set my king upon my holy hill of Zion."

The word "rage" is rather appropriate at this time in relationship to the Arab world. The media has reported on several occasions about the "day of rage."

However, it would be a grave mistake to apply the rage to the Arab people only. That is an error humanity has made throughout its 6,000 years of existence. It's always the other group, the other people, particularly the ones that are not like us.

The "rage" we are dealing with relates to the entire world. All the people of the earth are "imagining a vain thing."

> *It's always the other group, the other people, particularly the ones that are not like us.*

What is the purpose of their rage? What are they imagining? Verse 3 gives us the answer: "Let us break their bands asunder, and cast away their cords from us." That summarizes human history. Satan hates God. Why? Because God is love. Since all people of the world are subject to Satan, it stands to reason that humanity will and must oppose God's ordinances.

May we not be led astray by some noble sounding rhetoric, "We want peace, justice, and liberty for all." When such statements are made, the word "all" always means my group of people, my nation. What was and still is the result? The nations of the world fought against each other for millennia to establish their own imagined peace, liberty, prosperity, and justice for all.

But God Laughed

To the Lord in heaven, it is a bad joke, if we may say so. He laughs. God mocks at the thoughts, the plans, the imagination, and the rage of the people. In answer to the commotion of the world, God makes a very strange statement, "Yet have I set my king upon my holy hill of Zion."

In plain words, the answer is Zionism. We know who the King of Zion is. It is the Son of God, the Creator of heaven and earth, of whom the Psalmist exclaims, "Let Israel rejoice in him that made him: let the children of Zion be joyful in their King" (Psalm 149:2).

Jerusalem the Stumbling Stone

At the time of writing, our minds are occupied with the events taking place in the Arab world. Most of us do not fully realize what is happening in Zion, in Israel, in Jerusalem. When it comes to the issue of this city, the whole world is in a rage and the whole world is imagining a vain thing against Jerusalem.

There is not one nation that agrees with Scripture regarding Israel's geographical boundaries.

Almost 2,500 years ago, the prophet Zechariah proclaimed this to happen: "And in that day will I make Jerusalem a burdensome stone for all people: all that burden themselves with it shall be cut in pieces, though all the people of the earth be gathered together against it" (Zechariah 12:3). How very interesting: it is not just the Muslims, the atheists, the liberals, the communists, the socialists, the capitalists, but "all the people of the earth." There is not one nation that agrees with Scripture regarding Israel's geographical boundaries, nor does any nation agree to Jerusalem being the capital city of the Jewish state.

What to Expect in the Future

First of all, the invasion of democracy in Arab nations will bring the people who are the possessors of the world's largest energy sources into the camp of democratic prosperity.

We are not prognosticators, neither do we take it upon ourselves to speculate about the world's developments. But one thing we do know: we can place our total trust in the Word of God.

The times of the Gentiles began with Babylon some 2,600 years ago, and will end with Mystery Babylon, representing the entire world. While we have emphasized several times throughout this book that the real power lies in the invisible world, with the rulers of darkness, the spiritual wickedness in high places, yet the visible manifestation of these events must take place on earth, guided by the last Gentile power structure, Rome.

Our Hope

In view of the troubling events occurring on planet Earth, how is the Church expected to act? Are we to do everything in our power to hinder the development of the global world? To oppose world government? To reject a global currency? To fight against international laws? We may do so if we choose, but there is no Scripture to be found that confirms this to be the will of God for the Church.

The Church of Jesus Christ does not interfere in any way, shape or form. We who are born again of

His Spirit, are citizens of heaven, just passing through on our way to utterly indescribable glory.

We who are born again of His Spirit, are citizens of heaven, just passing through on our way to utterly indescribable glory.

Therefore, now more than ever, we do well to practice the instruction given by the Apostle Paul, inspired by the Holy Spirit: "Love worketh no ill to his neighbour: therefore love is the fulfilling of the law. And that, knowing the time, that now it is high time to awake out of sleep: for now is our salvation nearer than when we believed. The night is far spent, the day is at hand: let us therefore cast off the works of darkness, and let us put on the armour of light" (Romans 13:10-12).

ENDNOTES

Chapter 2

1 Wikipedia. 2011. "History of democracy." (http://en.wikipedia.org/wiki/History_of_democracy) Accessed 31 March 2011.
2 Ibid.
3 *Webster's New World College Dictionary.* 4th ed. 2002. Cleveland, OH: Wiley Publishing.
4 Ibid.
5 Reid, T.R. 1997. "The World According to Rome." *National Geographic.* August.
6 Ibid.
7 Froese, Arno. 2009. *Revelation Thirteen: Satan's Last Victory.* W. Columbia, SC: The Olive Press.
8 Pope Leo XIII. 1891. "The Condition of the Working Classes." *The Great Encyclical Letters of Pope Leo XIII.* May 15.
9 Andrews, Samuel J. 1898. *Christianity and Anti-Christianity in Their Final Conflict.* Chicago: Moody Press.
10 Ibid.
11 Ibid.
12 *Revelation Thirteen.*

Chapter 4

13 Smith, Tom W. and Seokho Kim. 2006. "National Pride in Comparative Perspective: 1995/96 and 2003/04." Chicago: NORC.

Chapter 5

14 United Nations. 2011. "Member States." (http://www.un.org/en/members/index.shtml) Accessed 31 March 2011.

15 Wikipedia. 2011. "Mapai." (http://en.wikipedia.org/wiki/Mapai) Accessed 17 May 2011.

16 Ibid.

Chapter 6

17 Froese, Arno. 1998. *Saddam's Mystery Babylon.* W. Columbia SC: The Olive Press.

Chapter 7

18 Nobelprize.org. "All Nobel Prizes." (http://nobelprize.org/nobel_prizes/lists/all/) Accessed 31 March 2011.

19 Hahn, Wilfred. 2005. *Eternal Value Review.* September.

20 Forbes.com. 2008. "Special Report: Islamic Finance." (http://www.forbes.com/2008/04/21/islamic-finance-sharia-islamic-finance-islamicfinance08-cx_ee_mn_0421islam_land.html) Accessed 19 April 2011.

21 NYTimes.com. 2010. "Born Somewhere Else." (http://www.nytimes.com/interactive/2010/06/27/weekinreview/27deparle-graphic.html?scp=1&sq=born%20somewhere%20else&st=cse) Accessed 17 May 2011.

22 *Rheinische Post.* 2010. "Pro-NRW-Aufmärsche: Islamfeinde sorgen für Aufruhr im Ruhrgebiet." 26 March. Translated by Arno Froese.

Chapter 10

23 Bureau of Labor Statistics. 2010. International Labor Comparisons. (http://www.bls.gov/fls/chartbook/section3.htm) Accessed 31 March 2011.

24 U.S. Energy Information Administration. 2008. International Energy Statistics. (http://www.eia.gov/cfapps/ipdbproject/IEDIndex3.cfm?tid=44&pid=44&aid=2) Accessed 31 March 2011.

25 Population Reference Bureau. *2008 World Population Datasheet.* (http://www.prb.org/pdf08/08WPDS_Eng.pdf) Accessed 31 March 2011.

26 Wikipedia. 2011. "Fuel tax." (http://en.wikipedia.org/wiki/Fuel_tax) Accessed 31 March 2011.

27 Ibid.

Chapter 11

28 Meacham, Jon. 2006. *American Gospel: God, the Founding Fathers, and the Making of a Nation.* New York: Random House.

29 Ibid.

30 Wikipedia. 2011. "Separation of church and state." (http://en.wikipedia.org/wiki/Separation_of_church_and_state) Accessed 31 March 2011.

Chapter 14

31 U.S. Geological Survey. 2011. Earthquake Facts and Statistics. (http://earthquake.usgs.gov/earthquakes/eqarchives/year/eqstats.php) Accessed 1 April 2011.

Chapter 15

32 Wikipedia. 2011. "Oil reserves." (http://en.wikipedia.org/wiki/Oil_reserves) Accessed 1 April 2011.

33 *The Economist.* 2011. "The Crescent and the Company." January 29.

34 Ibid.

Chapter 17

35 (http://travel.nationalgeographic.com/travel/countries/jordan-guide/) Accessed 9 June 2011.

36 The Arab Reform Initiative. *The State of Reform in the Arab World 2009-2010.* The Arab Democracy Index.

(http://www.social-sciences-and-humanities.com/PDF/annual_rep_010_english.pdf) Accessed 1 April 2011.

37 Amnesty International. Jordan—Amnesty International Report 2010. (http://www.amnesty.org/en/region/jordan/report-2010) Accessed 1 April 2011.

38 CIA World Factbook. 2011. (https://www.cia.gov/library/publications/the-world-factbook/) Accessed 1 April 2011.

39 (http://travel.nationalgeographic.com/travel/countries/lebanon-guide/) Accessed 9 June 2011.

40 CIA World Factbook.

41 (http://travel.nationalgeographic.com/travel/countries/syria-guide/) Accessed 9 June 2011.

42 CIA World Factbook.

43 (http://travel.nationalgeographic.com/travel/countries/egypt-guide/) Accessed 9 June 2011.

44 CIA World Factbook.

45 (http://travel.nationalgeographic.com/travel/countries/saudi-arabia-guide/) Accessed 9 June 2011.

46 CIA World Factbook.

47 World Economic Forum. *The Global Gender Gap Report 2010.* (http://www3.weforum.org/docs/WEF_GenderGap_Report_2010.pdf) Accessed 1 April 2011.

48 Serwer, Adam. 2010. "Understanding Islamic Finance." *The American Prospect.* (http://prospect.org/cs/articles?article=understanding_islamic_finance) Accessed 20 April 2011.

49 Ram, Vidya. 2008. Forbes.com. "The Enforcers." (http://www.forbes.com/2008/04/21/sharia-compliance-law-islamic-finance-islamicfinance08-cx_vr_0421 compliance.html) Accessed 1 April 2011.

INDEX

A

D

E

I

J

K

L

M

N

U

V

W

Y

Z

LIST OF FIGURES